Authentic Selling

How To Gain New Clients
Through Connection, Caring, and Service

By George Kao

Authentic Business Coach

www.GeorgeKao.com

This is an unusual Copyright Information page...

I, George Kao, give you permission to copy/paste any part of this book and share it anywhere online or offline, as long as you adhere to the license below.

CC0 1.0 Universal (CC0 1.0) -- Public Domain Dedication

No Copyright

The person who associated a work with this deed has dedicated the work to the public domain by waiving all of his or her rights to the work worldwide under copyright law, including all related and neighboring rights, to the extent allowed by law.

You can copy, modify, distribute and perform the work, even for commercial purposes, all without asking permission.

In no way are the patent or trademark rights of any person affected by CC0, nor are the rights that other persons may have in the work or in how the work is used, such as publicity or privacy rights.

Unless expressly stated otherwise, the person who associated a work with this deed makes no warranties about the work, and disclaims liability for all uses of the work, to the fullest extent permitted by applicable law.

When using or citing the work, you should not imply endorsement by the author or the affirmer.

Read more about the license here:
https://creativecommons.org/publicdomain/zero/1.0/

*It's important to me that these ideas get out into the world and implemented,
so that we might see more connection, caring, and deep service in the business world.*

--George Kao

Table of Contents

Section 1: The Mindset of Authentic Selling 1

Chapter 1: Instead of Selling, Work on Being of Service . 2

Before we continue, I'd love to know something about you. 6

Chapter 2: Authentic Marketing Metaphors 7

Chapter 3: When Does Selling Feel Scary? 13

Chapter 4: Instead of Persuasion, Work on Alignment .. 19

A Note for Paperback Readers 23

Chapter 5: A Better Way To Get More Attention 24

Chapter 6: Focus Your Marketing for Better Results 31

Chapter 7: The Core of Authentic Selling 38

Section 2: Your Audience & Your Offerings 44

Chapter 8: It's Never Too Early to Start Building an Audience 45

Chapter 9: Describing the Benefits of Your Services 51

Chapter 10: Memorizing Your Client Case Studies 58

Chapter 11: Describing the Mainstream Version of What You Do 61

Chapter 12: Authentic Pricing 65

Chapter 13: Twenty Ways to Improve Your Offerings ... 73

Chapter 14: Credibility Indicators for Your Services 81

Section 3: Ideas for Authentic Outreach 87

Chapter 15: How to Get Clients as an Authentic Business 88

Chapter 16: Need Clients ASAP? The Power of Personal Outreach 98

Chapter 17: Three Circles of Outreach 108

Chapter 18: Complimentary Call Launch 114

Chapter 19: How *Not* to Have a Sales Conversation .. 116

Chapter 20: More About Authentic Sales Conversations 124

Chapter 21: When Not Enough People are Signing Up 132

Section 4: Authentic Networking 141

Chapter 22: How to Keep in Touch with Previous Clients 142

Chapter 23: Seeking Referrals from Your Warm Connectors 147

Chapter 24: Who Are Your "Niche Mates"? 155

Chapter 25: Trading Content Promotions 162

Chapter 26: Trading Services for Feedback & Referrals 168

Chapter 27: Reaching Out to Group Owners/Admins . 173

Section 5: Pep Talk 176

Chapter 28: Your Outreach is a Blessing, not a Bother 177

Chapter 29: Consistent Income Requires Consistent Output 180

Chapter 30: To Go Big, Think Small 184

Chapter 31: Sell Only to Those Who Care 190

Can you tell me something about yourself? 196

Acknowledgements 197

About The Author 199

Section 1:

The Mindset of Authentic Selling

Chapter 1: Instead of Selling, Work on Being of Service

Have you ever heard that "sales is a numbers game"? According to that traditional idea, you just have to "pitch" your services to a lot of people, and some of them will become your clients.

A sales trainer might even tell you that "Every *no* means you are closer to a YES!"

If you've actually tried this, you'll know that it's brutal.

Trying to "sell" to a bunch of people is both intimidating and inauthentic as a way of connecting with others.

What if there was an alternative way to think about it, that felt more human and heart-centered… as well as being more effective?

Try this instead:

As you talk to people who might (or might not!) become your ideal clients, put yourself in the mode of understanding and helping them.

Try to find out the issues and challenges they're struggling with.

You probably know some person or resource that can be helpful to them.

In some cases, it turns out that *your* service is *exactly* what they need and want right now. If so, great! You can then say something like: "This is actually the kind of work I love doing with clients. If you're interested, I can give you more info."

But first, come to the conversation from an attitude of helping, being unattached to whether they ever hire you. This way, when it becomes apparent that they *want* your help, you can then simply share information and answer their questions, doing it all from a place of authentic helping.

When sales is only seen as a numbers game, you may have to talk to 100 people, and maybe you only get 3-10 new clients… which means 90-97 rejections. Even if you're an extraordinary salesperson and you convert 70 out of 100 people you're talking to, that's still 30 rejections. Nobody enjoys that.

Imagine all of that time spent trying to sell to people, to have to keep vigilant in those conversations for a bridge to start talking about your business. It feels inauthentic and exhausting.

Instead, when sales is seen as *a process of understanding and helping,* then you might still talk to 100 people, but the feeling is very different. You are genuinely *curious* about what they're going through and what kind of *help* they need, whether it's an idea, resource, tool, referral, or simply a kind listener.

You will then be occasionally delighted to discover that what they need at this time is *your* service or product. Let it be a surprise, rather than a planned, ulterior-motive ("I'm pretending to help you but I'm actually trying to sell you.")

Just help people.

As a result of your mindset shift, you'll no longer be churning through people, but instead you'll be serving everyone you connect with, bringing more light into their lives.

Serve, rather than sell.

It is a much more enjoyable process! And not surprisingly, some of the people you talk with, will want to come back to you as a resource, and perhaps become your client or referral source.

Whatever happens, you will be embodying the Golden Principle: Treat others with the kind of understanding and helping that you, too, would love to receive.

**Watch the companion video for this chapter here:
www.bit.ly/asbookvid1**

Before we continue, I'd love to know something about you.

One of the strange things about writing a book — instead of having a conversation — is that I don't know the person I'm "talking" to through this book.

Can you let me know a bit about you?

To help me with this, take a moment to fill out this short form:
www.GeorgeKao.com/BookSurvey

I personally read every response.

Upon submitting the form, you'll also see some bonus content related to this book!

Sincere Thanks,
George Kao

Chapter 2: Authentic Marketing Metaphors

In order to be able to do marketing and selling consciously (with awareness of how our actions impact others' emotions, as well as our own psyche), it is helpful to look at the foundational metaphors we use in marketing.

Here are the typical metaphors…

Marketing as War. You are waging a *campaign* to *crush* the competition, *undercut* them with lower prices, and *dominate* market share. (Many corporations use this metaphor.)

Marketing as Hunting. You are *baiting* your *target* audience into *capturing* their email address. As they buy a low price item, it is a *tripwire* that *triggers* your marketing funnel to sell them more, and hopefully, you'll *make a killing!* (This is the common metaphor used by digital marketers or internet marketers.)

Marketing as Religion. Structure your content to *indoctrinate* your new *followers* into your *worldview*, and eventually *convert* them into buyers. You'll have control over them when you become their *guru.* (This is essentially cult-building, trying to mind-control one's audience through hypnotic and persuasion techniques.)

Marketing as Science. Each piece of your content is an *experiment* to *test* the market for their *reactions* so you can keep adjusting for more *predictable results*. Don't get emotional about the ups or the downs. *Stay objective.* (I like this metaphor better than the others above, but using it exclusively means ignoring the heart, which will tend to erode a true relationship with your audience.)

Marketing as Dating. Just like it would be inappropriate to ask someone to marry you the first time you meet them, you don't ask your potential client to buy your biggest service package when they're just getting to know you. Ease them in, as you would in dating, through content and low-priced offers first. (This is a decent metaphor, because it's about human relationships. However, there are too many unethical or inauthentic dating methods out there. I'll offer a better metaphor below.)

So many marketers are unconscious of the metaphors they're using. They don't realize that they are spreading values in the world that *even they* would disagree with!

If there's dissonance between the marketer's higher values and their actions, the audience can sense it, making it difficult to build long-term trust. Also, the more that the marketer becomes conscious of this inner discord, the more he will sabotage his efforts, eventually causing a crisis in his business.

This is what happened to me in 2013. From 2009-2013, I was doing marketing actions that didn't align with my higher values. As I became more conscious of it, I began (unknowingly) to sabotage my own marketing efforts.

Eventually, I had to stop my business altogether. In 2014, I started over with a new way of being in business, a new metaphor for working with marketing that aligned with my higher values.

No longer was I doing war, hunting, or religion. I came to see marketing as education, service, and a cause—to help others (at scale) regardless of whether they bought from me.

I began to use a new metaphor: **Marketing as Friendship.**

I see myself building a friendship with my audience as a whole.

I start that friendship by connecting on common things, for example, our common interest in business based on higher values.

As a friend might do, I will keep in touch with you respectfully and only send you content that I truly believe you'll find helpful or interesting.

To know what is interesting for you, I stay observant in our interactions about your needs and wants. I learn about you more deeply so that I can better help you.

If I think you are misguided about something, I'm not going to judge you. I will still respect and care for you. Of course, I will try to share my way of thinking, to see if it also resonates with you.

Importantly, I also listen to your opinions and allow the possibility for *you* to change my perspective, to modify or upgrade my point of view.

Growing up, my mother told me *"Everyone will say nice things to you. Your real friends are willing to tell you the hard truths, in hopes that it may help you."* Similarly, I sometimes ask you to be honest with me on how I can improve. I am observant of any suggestions I get from you.

Of course, not everyone will resonate with me as a friend, and similarly, I don't expect everyone to resonate with my marketing.

A compatible friend would totally accept me as I am. Similarly, I feel liberated in my marketing to be myself, knowing that the audiences that are meant for me *will* resonate with my content and style. I encourage you to think that way about your own content and style as well.

I can only have a limited number of friends before I start forgetting important details about them. Similarly, I am not looking to become a celebrity. I just want a sustainable number of clients, and an organically growing number of readers that I can keep up with. I might gradually build a small team of assistants, but I will always try to personally get to know at least some of my fans, as representatives of my audience, so I can keep being as relevant and helpful to my audience as I can.

Friends meet new friends through introductions. This is the best way that marketing happens as well: spreading goodness through word-of-mouth.

Friendship is based on trust. So in my marketing I will always work to maintain your trust, never trying to "get" you to do something that feels *off* to you or to me.

Just like you would start to distance yourself from a friend who was always trying to sell stuff to you, I will always serve more with free content, and only occasionally sell.

In my selling, it's more like I'm inviting a friend to a party, an experience together. It's something we do to bond more, and to further our growth.

Also, sometimes friends drift apart for awhile. Similarly, I'm ok if you stop reading my stuff and go hang out with other marketers you resonate with. When you do come back to our friendship, you'll be the richer for it. The bottom line is that I don't try to keep you as a friend, because *good friends are not pushy or needy.*

This old saying is so true, especially in marketing: *"If you love them, let them go."* I hold loosely to having to *get* and *keep* your attention. I simply serve as a loyal friend, continually learning more about you (my audience) and bonding with you through our interactions.

These are ideas that I'm not yet perfect at implementing, yet I practice and aspire to be.

Thank you for your support and friendship.

Watch the companion video for this chapter here: www.bit.ly/asbookvid2

Chapter 3: When Does Selling Feel Scary?

There's actually just one situation when you are afraid to sell your services...

...when you don't believe the transaction is truly a win-win.

On the other hand, if you really believe in your services, and know that the person you're talking to would find it to be a great deal at the price you're offering, then you're no longer afraid to sell.

It becomes almost a cause to let them know about it.

Think about it: When you're excited by a service you've used and loved, it's so easy to tell a friend that they would also love it. You take pride in informing your friends about a great deal for them.

It feels like an act of generosity.

Why don't you feel that way about your own services?

Problem 1: You don't really believe your service is worth the price you're charging for it.

Here are some solutions:

(A) You can improve your service until you believe it's worth the current price. This is a worthy, and longer-term solution. It takes time to improve your skills. Getting some coaching in your field will speed that along.

(B) You can lower your price for now, until you feel like your service is an excellent deal.

As a result of a more accessible price, more people will give your services a try, which gives you the opportunity for more practice, thereby allowing you to improve your skills more quickly.

(There's a common myth being perpetuated out there: "When you raise your rates, you'll get more clients." Again and again, in my own and others' experience, I have not found that to be true. There are always exceptions, but I wouldn't recommend raising your rates when you're already having a hard time getting enough clients.)

After awhile, you'll start feeling like you're charging too little for all the real benefit you're giving to your clients, and you'll feel a natural pull to increase your prices. This is the right time to do so.

(C) You can create a lower-price service or product that makes it easier for people to say yes to trying out your expertise.

☙

Problem 2: You don't know your audience well enough to feel confident that they would find your services to be a great deal.

Some solutions:

(A) Have more 1-1 conversations with your audience. Start with the ones who are supportive of you, who are already engaging with your content. (This is why I'm such a fan of authentic content marketing, and why I wrote my first book about it.)

Ask them to tell you: what services or programs similar to yours they have bought or are considering buying and most importantly, the reasons they are considering it.

Ask them to give you honest suggestions about how you can improve your services to genuinely feel like a really good deal, that it's definitely affordable and a great match for them or friends they can think of.

Remember: "I can't afford this" often means "Even though I *can* afford it, it's not the right match for me yet."

(B) You can change the audience you're selling to. (Not necessarily change it for good, but try reaching out to new audiences with this service/product.)

You can do this by using Facebook Ads skillfully to reach audiences that might be better match for your services. I teach a whole course about how to do that here: www.GeorgeKao.com/FacebookWorkshop

However, before you try *selling* to a new audience, it's a good idea to build trust with them first. Do this by advertising your best free content for a little while. In other words, start with authentic content marketing.

Another way to find new audiences is by seeking out some current or new colleagues who do not provide the same services as you do, but who have an audience who might love your services. This could be fellow coaches, experts, bloggers, FB group owners, LinkedIn group owners, or others who have an email newsletter.

When reaching out to colleagues to ask them to promote your services, the same principle I've named above applies: the only time it's scary is when you don't really believe the transaction is a win-win.

Therefore:

(1) Make sure your incentive for your colleague is so good that they will find it a great deal.

For example, share enough percentage of commissions that they can see you are being generous.

And/or give them some free sessions of your services (or a generous sample of your product) so they can benefit and truthfully endorse and promote your work.

(2) Research your colleague's content and audience in advance, before contacting them, so that you feel confident that their audience would love your services, and that it would be appropriate (based on their content) for them to share you with their audience.

Then as you contact your colleague, you may want to give a link to a few pieces of your best content (choose something similar to what you're asking them to promote) so they can see what a good fit this partnership could be.

To summarize:

Selling (or networking) is scary only when you haven't done the homework of making that promotion or conversation a true win-win. Do the homework. Follow the tips above, so that it no longer feels like selling, but instead, a feel-good activity of connecting in a truly win-win way. Let it become a joyful cause!

**Watch the companion video of this chapter here:
www.bit.ly/asbookvid3**

Chapter 4: Instead of Persuasion, Work on Alignment

Do you enjoy having to convince or persuade people to buy from you?

Persuasion sets up an arms-folded, you vs. me dynamic.

I'd like to present you with an alternative:

*Instead of trying to sell, let's do our best to **align** with our potential clients.*

In selling, it is typically assumed that you must learn persuasion tactics.

Persuasion strategies do work... but only for the short-term.

When a buyer has to be persuaded during the sales process, they often later regret the purchase. As the seller, you lose a long-term customer, and probably get some negative word-of-mouth reputation, whether you become aware of it or not.

As consumers, all of us have been tricked by persuasive selling, and we have felt buyer's remorse. Persuasion tactics tend to short-circuit our own natural buying process, which has its own rhythm and timing and needs to be respected.

Our conscience is saying, "There's got to be a better way."

Instead of trying to persuade someone to buy, we can instead work to align what we offer with the people who need and want what we have.

1. We are in selling alignment when we offer the right thing to the right person, at the right time, for the right price. When we fail to align on any of those, we become needy or desperate, and fall back into persuasion tactics.

2. To find alignment, we need to talk with enough prospective customers in the right way—to understand what problems they really want to solve that our service can help with and to discover what they and their friends buy that is similar to our service.

3. We need to keep improving our services and our understanding of whom it's best for, so that we can talk about our services honestly and transparently. When we know what our services do and whom they help, we feel energized to take our services to the people who really need it. When we approach selling from this service-oriented way, with care and love for our ideal audience, we find sales alignment. We no longer need to persuade. We

can just whisper our offers, and our ideal customers will love to buy from us.

~~~
Let's say that what you sell is an ointment for foot fungus. Stay with me here. If you're presenting your ointment to someone who has foot fungus, or a close friend who suffers from it, then you don't have to do any selling or persuasion. If the price is similar to other types of ointments they've seen, and they (or a close friend) has that very problem, then there's alignment between the buyer and the product.

However, if you are talking to someone who doesn't have foot fungus and doesn't know anyone with that problem, but *your* goal is to make the sale, to meet your numbers, then you will become desperate or otherwise use persuasion tactics such as "Listen to these scary stories of people who had foot fungus… you *might* develop it too, so you better buy it now. Last chance at this price! You'll never see this great offer again!"

Bottom line: In your marketing, selling, networking, and copywriting, remember that persuasion is only necessary when you don't really understand the other person. If however you want to build business from a space of caring, then work instead on finding alignment.

This chapter's companion video: www.bit.ly/asbookvid4

A Note for Paperback Readers

Starting in the next chapter you'll see some phrases underlined. These are hyperlinks that are clickable in the *electronic* copy of the book.

If you purchased a new copy of this paperback via Amazon, you can get the e-book (Kindle) version **for free**, through Amazon's Kindle Matchbook program. Here's how:

1. Log into your Amazon.com account
2. Search and find this book on Amazon
3. Click on the Kindle version. If you purchased this paperback through your Amazon account, you should be able to get the Kindle version for free.

With the Kindle version you'll be able to click on the hyperlinks in this book.

Enjoy!

~ George Kao

Chapter 5: A Better Way To Get More Attention

In marketing it is assumed that the goal is to get more views, followers, and sales.

The goal is to get others to do what **we** want **them** to do.

"If I don't strive to get my share of attention, I won't be able to survive and shine."

This can easily spiral into "by any means necessary." There are plenty of questionable marketing strategies and pushy sales tactics that will "get" you more audience attention and action. The reason people keep doing it is because it works in the short term.

Eventually, it always comes back to haunt them, but it's because it's delayed into the future, they're blind to it now.

It's this "I want you to do this for me" focus that makes us consumers distrust and dislike so much of marketing. It's so salesy or pushy—whether it's the emails we get, or the calls to actions at the end of posts or videos. We feel we have to consume marketing, in order to get to the good stuff—the content we actually want.

Additionally, so many ads and commercials are annoying because it doesn't really speak to our wants or needs. Marketers don't care enough—they're just blasting their message to everyone, hoping to catch a few, and not caring enough to slow down and really understand and target their advertising thoughtfully. It feels interruptive, a necessary evil, which is why ad blockers are so popular.

Instead of "how can we get more attention," what if we think in terms of "how can we care more?"

In <u>authentic business</u>, we are being called to bring *more love* and *more wisdom* into business. That is the core focus.

Rather than always "more attention" and "more sales" let us focus on "more care."

By expanding our level of care for our audience, we also tend to receive increased attention, happier customers, and natural word of mouth sharing.

When we care more for our current readers, our existing clients, and our own network, we grow a deeper understanding of them. We can then create content and offerings that are more relevant to them.

Everybody wins.

Do You Care Enough to Seek Conversation?

We need to care so much about our audience that we become eager to get to know them better. What are they thinking about? How do they feel about our industry or the offerings we provide? What can we do to meet them where they actually are, to serve them better?

Willingness to care means willingness to talk to them. To converse one to one with as many people in our audience as possible. To reach out privately to the engagers of our content and social media. To individually contact some of our email subscribers and get to know them.

Not just sending out surveys, but caring enough to be in one to one conversation with them.

In our conversations, try to uncover what it is they're struggling with now, in ways that we are able to help. Try to find out what related products or services they've bought but aren't totally satisfied with and therefore what products we might create (or curate).

Most of us business owners are so in our own heads (and hearts), absorbed with our own peak experiences, in love with our own modality, focused on promoting our own ideas, that we can easily lose touch with what the audience actually wants and cares about.

We need to care about our audience more than our possible embarrassment by their silence or rejection. Let's get out of self-centeredness and get more curious and audience-centered.

Let's keep returning to these questions:

How can I care more for my audience?

How can I better understand them?

How can I show care in a way that they can see and feel?

This is how real trust and loyal attention are created. Not by trying to *grab* attention, but by caring so much that others naturally begin to trust and express loyalty to you.

How Are You Spending Your Time?

Are you working on perfecting your website even after it is past the point of being functional and user friendly? Then you might be spending more time caring about preserving a high self-image of yourself than serving your audience.

A better approach might be to spend time doing website user interviews so that the improvements you make are benefiting the actual concerns of your audience instead of the ones in your head.

Another example: if you want to create an online course, are you spending a long time on preparing it with little or no audience feedback? Again, you may be in your head too much. How do you know what your audience actually wants? I always launch courses by selling the outline (in the form of a sales page) first, and then if there are enough students, I then create the course module by module while the students are taking it, so that I can get their real-time feedback to make the next module what they want and need. That way, the course can be truly relevant for them. I change the course outline as needed, to meet the students where they're at.

Are you spending years trying to write a book? Have you considered writing it in chunks while incorporating reader feedback? What I do is blog each week on Medium, study the response, and organize the best blog posts into an upcoming book. This way, I am putting together a book based on content that my audience cares about, not just swimming in my own thoughts.

The bottom line is that so many of us are in-our-head with our marketing actions. We are not doing enough true productivity in our authentic business—taking the action of being in conversation with other human beings.

So many entrepreneurs want to become influencers. They think that "getting more attention" is the way to get there.

The problem is that there is only so much attention that can go around.

When you are reading my content, you can't simultaneously be reading someone else's. When someone is watching your video, they aren't at the same time consuming someone else's.

Therefore most influencers compete by trying to be more entertaining, shocking, and clever with their calls-to-action, to become a fan, subscribe to their channel, to buy their products.

Instead of trying to be more entertaining, clever, and competitive, let's spend our energies on being more caring.

I dream of a world where influencers truly care and have deeper engagement with the true fans who support them. Instead of trying to get millions of followers, focus on caring for your true fans, and your business will thrive.

Share this chapter, or to comment on it, using this link:
https://medium.com/@georgekao/want-more-attention-care-more-than-others-do-54da2c7a3683

Chapter 6: Focus Your Marketing for Better Results

When you start to learn marketing, you're going to get pulled in many different directions. Which way should you go? What should you do first?

One expert: "You must do video, and upload it to Youtube & Facebook!"

Another expert: "It's all about connecting with Instagram influencers."

Yet another expert: "The fastest way to build an email list is by organizing a Telesummit!"

An SEO expert: "None of the above builds you a truly long-term asset unless you're posting SEO-focused articles to your blog regularly!"

Who do you believe?

Running in Circles

The truth: Progress in any positive direction -- taken far enough -- yields vast treasures. When you go farther than the majority of people, in any good direction, you get larger benefits than most people will.

Imagine you're on a journey. You follow one expert's guidance and go North for awhile. Then, a shiny strategy in the West makes you do a 90-degree left-turn and you go there for some time. Then you realize that the treasures of the NorthEast are far more worthwhile to you, so you take a sharp right turn. Then, a friend that you deeply trust, says she's getting great results in the South, so you do another sharp right turn.

You're essentially going in a big circle.

No matter how fast you move, if you do any big turns, you've lost the momentum of the original direction.

Persistence in any one direction = Excellence.

There's a profound compound effect in skill-building. The more consistently you do something, the better you get at it, faster.

For years, I wrote only once in awhile. And for years, I hated to write every time, and wasn't very good at it.

3 years ago, I committed to writing multiple times a week. To this day, I'm still consistent with this habit. I've grown in

my writing skills more quickly in the past 3 years than in the previous 30 years.

Fits and starts = painfully slow skill-building.

Apply this to your business and marketing: are you following one strategy for a month, and then you get bored—or see a shiny new strategy—and chase a new thing?

If so, you're not giving yourself the chance to become deeply skillful at any one strategy. No wonder you're struggling to get results.

You don't have to be everywhere.

You can grow a thriving business with any ONE platform… if you become excellent at it.
Whether it's Facebook, Youtube, Podcasts, Instagram, Medium, Twitter, Pinterest, or Linkedin. If you choose one, learn and practice it well enough to become a pro, your business will see results.

Unless you're a generalist marketing expert (like me), you don't have to be on multiple social media platforms, and be doing different marketing strategies.

What if you get bored?

For any one marketing platform you choose, there is so much to learn. You get bored only if you aren't pushing yourself to new heights on that platform.

Keep observing the people who are excellent at it. What can you learn from them? When was the last time you took an advanced class about that platform? Or at least watched some Youtube videos about the best current strategies?

Eliminate boredom by deeper exploration of that one platform you've chosen.

Which Platform To Choose?

Which platform are you intrigued by and enjoy learning about?

Which platform has your ideal audience on it?

If you could only choose one platform to become excellent at, what would it be?

Write down your answers to the above questions. Is there a platform or strategy that shows up in all of the answers?

If there's still more than one option, use a [randomizer tool](#) to help you select one. When the random answer comes up, were you happy about it? Or were you secretly hoping for a different option? There you have your answer.

Know that any of the major platforms -- Facebook, Youtube, Podcasts, Instagram, Medium, Twitter, Linkedin, Pinterest -- has hundreds of millions of people, out of which probably tens of thousands are your ideal clients, more than your business will ever need.

Focus to win.

Don't try to learn everything before choosing one.

The perfectionist will say: "Yes, but I need to take courses in all the available platforms, do my due diligence, before settling on one."

Do you realize how long that will take you? Maybe hundreds of hours. And then, just when you think you've learned them all, you'll come across 5 other platforms or strategies you didn't even realize existed until that moment.

It's a never-ending cycle.

Instead, if you just choose one and then spend the time applying yourself in that one direction, you'll get business results more quickly. And if you focus your curiosity on that one platform, there's never ending things to learn there, always new ways to get better at it.

If I were to choose only one...

...I would choose Facebook for marketing.

Of all the platforms I've tested, Facebook (especially using ads) has made it the easiest to reach the most number of the right people, simply because it's three to five times larger than other platforms. Despite the recent scandals, it's still where most people are. And Facebook usership is <u>still growing</u>.

I don't really use Facebook to post about my personal life, what I'm eating, or who I'm hanging out with. 95% of my time on Facebook is spent on <u>my business page</u>.

This is why of all the social media platforms I could teach, I decided to focus on <u>Facebook Marketing Training</u>.

Even two modes of content (writing and video) might be more than you might need to do. I'm a content expert, so it makes sense for me to do more in my field.

If you are feeling stretched for time and energy, focus on just one content format, so you can become better at it much more quickly. That's where the best results are.

Share this chapter, or to comment on it, using this link:
https://www.georgekao.com/blog/focusyourmarketing

Chapter 7: The Core of Authentic Selling

I see authentic selling as the natural extension of an authentic approach to business. When we truly care for our audience and customers, and take actions to show them, we build genuine trust that naturally leads to sales.

However, the more attached we are to the results of our marketing or selling, the more inauthentic it can become.

"Results-driven marketing" can easily lead into manipulation.

If we "must" get a particular result, we become manipulative of others and the situation. *And if the result doesn't happen, we experience inner suffering.*

Instead, when we focus our energy on **inner-exploration** and **outer-service**, then our marketing becomes authentic. No matter the result, we can enjoy the activity. Our marketing becomes not only authentic, but also sustainable.

Let me explain:

Most marketing is tied to ROI (return on investment).

Yet:

Marketing that is creative or innovative (by definition: doing something new) cannot accurately predict the ROI.

So there's this illusion that you're supposed to be able to Do X and get Y results. I send this cleverly-copywritten email and get $1,000 in sales. I buy $1,000 of Facebook Ads and I get $2,500 in revenue.

If you're growing an authentic business, you know that it rarely works in such predictable ways.

You're in business to express your soul and serve others' positive transformation.

You're not in business primarily to get money, right? (If you were, you should be in the finance industry instead.) You're doing your business because of a calling. And, you know this:

If you're faithful to your business calling, which includes serving others in ways they want, then healthy money is **a natural result.**

Yet when we start learning business and marketing from experts, they often assume that we're in business primarily to make money. The way they get our attention is always something like "Get more traffic and profits!" and "Build a 6-figure income!"

They've made money the god of their business.

They're doing marketing for the sales, not for the joy.

Therefore, the mode of operation is manipulation.

The natural result is cycles of short-term highs (when campaigns are profitable) and suffering (when a campaign doesn't meet its intended results).

If we learn marketing from such experts, we also become attached to results.

We start to see marketing as a means to an end. Marketing becomes a necessary evil, to build a business that we want.

Compromising your values isn't going to build a business that fulfills you.
I'm here to present a different path, one that can feel more true to the heart.

Just like business can be a calling, so can marketing be a soulful expression.

Instead of "do X so that you can get Y" (a means to an end), what if X itself was worth doing, regardless of whether you get Y?

That's how I see marketing—when done authentically, marketing is an activity that is worthwhile in and of itself.

Authentic marketing is the intersection of the exploration of one's soul and one's genuine service to the world.

It is not "so that I can get more traffic and make more sales"… although that may be a result.

When you share your authentic expression in service to the world, others can sense your authenticity. That is where real trust begins to build. Trust is where solid sales are made.

Yet if you focus on the sale, you'll eventually lose their trust.

So it's really about where you focus your attention as you do your marketing and outreach: on the soulful expression or on the results?

During the marketing itself: be in the authenticity of exploration, expression, and service.

After the marketing is over, with some distance of time, we can then look at the outer results—how the audience responded—in order to tune our marketing intuition to better serve the audience next time.

When you are doing any of your marketing—whether it's your article writing, your video creation, your web page development, your email sending, your advertising design, your webinars, your conversations with prospective clients—may something like this be your inner mantra:

Bless and Let Go.

Be in service to your ideal audience, knowing that even your marketing itself is an offering.

Not that I'm perfect in following this principle. I write this as a reminder to myself. Neither are my clients perfect, but we are always aiming for joy.

I wish for all of us the ability to do our marketing from a deep place of trust, seeing it as <u>work we do from an inner spark of joy</u>, so that we can be joyfully sustainable in our marketing.

And if we are sustainable in doing the activity of marketing, it is inevitable that we get business results. Persistence truly pays off.

Yet rather than persisting from a place of "hustle" (hardship), and "I'm only doing this as a means to an end" (necessary evil), let's transform our relationship to the activity of marketing: make it worthwhile in itself.

Let marketing be an exploration of your authenticity and a genuine offering of service to your audience.

Then no matter what you can enjoy your business.

Watch the companion video of this chapter here: www.bit.ly/asbookvid7

Section 2:

Your Audience & Your Offerings

Chapter 8: It's Never Too Early to Start Building an Audience

A regret that many entrepreneurs have is that they didn't start building their audience sooner.

If you think you might want to start a business one day, I recommend that you start growing your audience now.

But how do you start?

- As you come across any idea that is interesting or helpful to you, share it on social media (whichever platform you use).
- As you read an article or book that you find interesting or helpful, write a quick summary of it and post it on social media.
- As you watch and find a video you really like, share it, and say why it's worth watching.
- If there's something you disagree with, be sure to say why—start building your muscles in saying what you believe.
- If you have a sense of what your passion is, or what your future business might be, start a Facebook Business Page right away. Just use your own name—build your personal brand—you can always change your page name later.

- Start posting content about your passion, whether it's sharing other people's content, or as you get more courageous and creative, start posting your own content. Remember <u>the 3 stages of content</u>: exploration, repurposing, and finally monetization.

Whatever you do, start now.

Whichever social media platform you choose doesn't really matter: Facebook, Youtube, Instagram, Medium, iTunes (podcasting), Linkedin, Twitter, Pinterest, Tumblr. The question is: which platform do you enjoy using? Start there. *Any of these* are big enough to build an audience.

Then, when you are ready in the future to promote a product, message, or cause, you will have an audience there to receive it, who already know and trust you!

The Fantasy of "Instant Promotion"

Some business owners have the fantasy of "instant promotion"—that they will be able to gain buyers for their product or service right away... when they have no audience to begin with.

Instant promotion only works if:

- You sell a very mainstream service, something that many people already buy, e.g. tax preparation.
- You have the means to start with a large advertising budget, e.g. $1,000 per month.

If, instead, you have a non-mainstream service (life coach, relationship counselor, transformational facilitator, etc.) and you only have maybe a $50/month advertising budget, then you need to start building your audience as soon as possible.

Don't expect to wait until you're "ready" to sell something, and then assume you'll *just* post it on Facebook or tweet it out, and clients will show up.

If no one knows who you are, no one's going to buy from you.

Good copywriting and branding won't save you either.

Maybe you think—"I'll just hire a copywriter or marketing expert. They'll help me create amazing messaging and branding. " This is yet another fantasy.

I've seen it again and again: if it is not tied to the relationship you have with your existing audience and the feedback you get from them, then even amazing messaging and branding can be a huge disappointment and a big waste of time and money.

If, however, you build an audience first, and then you get to know them and base your marketing message & branding on what you've observed about them, you will then be able to get clients, and without using manipulative marketing.

What it means to have an audience:

1. You've been sharing helpful content on social media, and you notice that you have several dozen people who engage with your content on a regular basis.
2. Or you're a good networker, and have dozens of friends and colleagues that you have supportive relationships with, who are likely to promote your business when it's time to do so.

Ideally you have both, but start at least one of these efforts as soon as possible.

My preferred method is <u>authentic content marketing</u>, which is in a nutshell, building an audience around your "personal brand" (your name, your thoughts, your authentic style) so that you can be flexible, and pivot to having any kind of business you want in the future.

Don't wait until you figure out what your niche is.

This is a fantasy:

- Figure out your business idea or niche → Promote it and get customers

(Unless you have a very mainstream service, and a large advertising budget.)

Reality works more like this:

- Build an audience → Get to know them → Create your marketing message and offerings based on what resonates with them → Get customers/clients

I've written about this here: <u>Are you trying to define your niche too early?</u>

Before you figure out your niche, start creating a network/audience for your personal brand now.

Given the rapid growth of artificial intelligence and automation, <u>humans will have an increasingly hard time finding a job</u>.

If you develop entrepreneurial skills, and build your own audience, you'll be in a much better position to create your own job, your own livelihood, your own meaningful work, instead of hoping someone will give you a job.

For everyone who wants meaningful work in the future, it is imperative to start building your own audience now.

It's like the old saying...

When's the best time to have planted a tree?
10 years ago.

When's the next best time?
Today.

This is true of your personal brand as well.

Your audience and brand don't have to take ten years to build. But if you start today, you will be in a much better position one year from now.

Share this chapter, or to comment on it, using this link:
https://www.georgekao.com/blog/startaudiencenow

Chapter 9: Describing the Benefits of Your Services

If you're trying to sell a service, for example coaching or healing, you might hear from marketing experts that you should never sell the method (how you do it) but always sell the benefits and always speak to your ideal client.

But you're left wondering—"how do I know *which* benefits people really care about… and *what type of person* is my ideal client?"

To answer these questions, you need to:

1. Be taking notes about client sessions as you have them.
2. Work with different types of people, so that more individuals experience your modality and so you can see for whom your skills are most valuable and in what situations.

Let me talk about each of these.

Doing More of Your Work

If you haven't done your work for many different types of people, you are limiting yourself. You don't know how your process affects different people.

There's a "secret" that experienced service providers know: the more ideal the client is, the better their results.

In other words, it's not just about *you* improving your skills. Even with the same skills, one client will get dramatically better results, and another client gets very little results.

The determining factor? The kind of client you're working with.

In the beginning, when you simply need work, you're happy to accept any person who wants to be your client. That's good, because you then get to experience a variety of personalities and situations.

If you are looking to do more of your work, try <u>trading with other service providers for feedback</u>.

But it is equally important to take notes after each client session for the purpose of understanding where your skills are most valuable, and to whom.

Taking Notes

"The palest ink is better than the strongest memory."
(Chinese proverb)

When trying to describe your service, or the benefits of what you provide, or who your ideal client is, do you just "go by intuition" or do you "try to remember"?

It's more accurate and easier when you have notes to look at, so that you can see the actual patterns and commonalities between your best clients (those who get the most results with you)— and your "worst" clients (those who get the least results).

Get into the habit of taking notes after each client session:

1. What success or benefits have they experienced, since their previous session with you? (If this is the first session, skip to question 3.)
2. What did you do that helped them to get this benefit/success? What part did you play?
3. For the session you just completed: What problem did they come to the session with?
4. What was the "aha! moment" or the biggest benefit that the client experienced?

5. What did you do in this session that helped them the most? What exercise, process, or idea did you share with them?

If you answer the above questions right after each client session, and do this on a consistent basis, you will start to notice patterns. And it will help you describe your services more accurately, and to write more authentic marketing copy.

Another benefit: you'll be getting new and relevant ideas for your content.

If it's been a long time or you haven't been doing this, I would not recommend taking notes as it can all meld together in your mind. <u>Every time we access a particular memory, it actually changes.</u> You might be making things up.

Just start today with your note-taking and go forward from there.

Who are your ideal clients?

In addition to post-session notes, it's also helpful to take overall notes about each client.
When the client first starts to work with you:

1. Demographics e.g. their age, gender, profession, field of study (helpful if you run FB ads)—you can find this info on their Facebook or LinkedIn profile.
2. How they found you. Be specific: which post or ad did they see (if they remember)? Which friend or colleague referred them to you? (If possible, reach out with gratitude to that referral source.) What were they searching for online that allowed them to come across your site?
3. What they are looking for. What motivated them to seek out your services? What problem or goal or situation?
4. What they've already tried. What solution or service have they already tried, before working with you? What hasn't worked well for them, and why? (This helps you to see what gaps are in the market that your service can fill, and that you can emphasize in your marketing.)

When the client completes a package of sessions with you:
1. What results or benefits came from the work with you?
2. How much did they spend on your services & products?
3. Give them a private rating (for your eyes only). Example:
    - 0 = totally ineffective or high-maintenance client.
    - 3 = average client.
    - 5 = extraordinarily effective and easy to work with.
    - Note—we are not rating them "as a person" obviously, but only about how good a fit they happened to be, at this time, with your service.
4. Reasons for Rating. If a poor rating, was it the wrong time in their life to be using your service? Or did they have the wrong idea about what the service is? How can you improve your marketing to filter out the less-ideal clients? If it was a great rating, what was it about this client or their situation? Can you talk more about that in your marketing?
5. What's next for them? What are they needing next? This may give you ideas to form referral

partnerships, or to create an additional service if it doesn't dilute your focus.

Look for patterns with every batch of clients that you take these notes about (e.g. every 10 clients). What type of client gets your highest rating? What type gets your lowest rating?

(If you seek out patterns with too few clients, you may be analyzing an unusual case rather than a true pattern.)

Stay open to working with a wide range of client types and situations, until you see a clear pattern of what type of client situation is best—and worst—for your service.

Then, modify your marketing to speak directly to the ideal client, and to filter out the less-ideal clients.

Share this chapter, or to comment on it, using this link:
https://medium.com/@georgekao/how-to-describe-what-you-do-who-are-your-ideal-clients-take-notes-after-client-sessions-a6b26c944f46

Chapter 10: Memorizing Your Client Case Studies

The exercise that follows will help with your marketing, as well as improve the relevancy of your services to your clients:

Step 1. Take out the notes you took about your clients, based on the previous chapter. (If you haven't worked with any clients yet, then you'll need to imagine your ideal client: Bring them into your mind and heart.)

Step 2. Now, write a quick story that answers these questions:

a. What problems are they facing as they begin to work with you? What challenges have caused them to seek you out? What hopes or dreams do they believe they can achieve by working with you?

b. What work are you doing with them? What method are you using to support them? What tools, exercises, processes do you give them?

c. What are their reactions and insights? Is there something they were initially confused by, then became enlightened about? When did they have the greatest "aha!" moment, in working with you? What part of the work did they love most?

d. What is the result or transformation they'll get from working with you? Describe specifics. Imagine a movie of their life, before and after working with you. What does the contrast look like? Give details that illustrate that transformation.

NOTE: The story doesn't have to be perfect, nor have great grammar, nor be very compelling. Just write something down for now. You can always improve upon it later!

Step 3. After finishing that story, start writing another one.

Aim to write 5 or more such stories, of various clients. These could be actual current clients, past clients, or imaginary future clients.

Step 4. Pick the 3 stories that most energize you.

Step 5. Find the common threads among these stories, for example:

a. Issues they originally came to you for

b. Solutions you used

c. Results they gained

Step 6. Memorize the stories and the common threads. This will be very useful whenever you work on your marketing, or when you're describing your service to someone.

Share this chapter, or to comment on it, using this link: https://www.facebook.com/GeorgeKaoCommunity/posts/10154801588904867/

Chapter 11: Describing the Mainstream Version of What You Do

What's the mainstream version of what you do?

When should someone seek you out?

Your prospective clients don't need to know the nuances of your field.

If you're an energy healer, they don't need to know that there are 15 different modalities (or whatever).

If you're a relationship counselor, they don't need to know that there are 8 different philosophies.

If you're a life coach, they don't need to know that there are 5 major life coaching schools and why the one you graduated from is different from the rest.

Your prospective clients don't value the nuances that you spent years immersed in.

Talk only about the things they understand and value. Describe your service in a way that they can easily "get"...

For example, energy healing: how is that different from what normal physicians do? Would you state that conventional doctors work on the physical body only, unaware of any level beyond, and use what are sometimes intrusive methods that can have bad side effects? Instead, does an energy healer work on the subtle spiritual level that strengthens the body's power to heal itself?

Secondly, when does someone ideally seek out energy healing vs. the mainstream doctors? Perhaps after a patient has gone through invasive surgery and needs the body to heal more quickly? Or in conjunction with chemotherapy, so the body and emotions can be supported at a profound level, so as to not break down? Or before a physical problem gets so bad that conventional medicine becomes the last resort?

I encourage you to answer these 3 questions:

1. What's the mainstream version of what you do, that people can easily understand?

2. How are you different from that mainstream version?

3. At what point should your ideal client seek you out? Sometimes you are not a substitute to mainstream, but instead you might be a complement to what the mainstream

does. (This is why alternative medicine is often called "complementary medicine.")

You're welcome to comment at the bottom of [this Facebook thread](#) with your answers, if you'd like.

My own example:

I'm an alternative to the typical internet marketing expert. They teach quick profits which are unreliable and unrealistic, and often to the detriment of the long-term trust and viability of one's audience, business, health, relationship, and spiritual integrity…

Prospective clients seek me out after they have become turned off by that conventional, money-driven marketing expert and their strategies… and unfortunately, after some of them have been taken for thousands of dollars by buying other programs and trainings.

By the time they come to me, they've gotten wiser as to what business strategies they don't resonate with (even if those strategies *sound* amazing), and now, are less likely to be sucked in again by those methods. They are seeking an alternative that feels true, that is deeply aligned with their integrity and sense of service.

In summary, I'm a marketing consultant (mainstream title) who helps service providers gain new clients (mainstream benefit) through conscious and heart-based methods (what makes me unique from the mainstream). Clients love working with me after they've realized that typical marketing methods don't feel aligned with their higher purpose (this is when clients seek me out).

Now it's your turn to answer the questions above, and come up with your summary. Once you do, share it with your friends & supportive colleagues, and see if they have any suggestions.

Use their feedback to improve your description, until it's so concise and simple to understand that people can easily refer your services to others in a typical conversation.

You can see how some other people answered the above questions, and add your own, at the bottom of this Facebook thread.

Chapter 12: Authentic Pricing

Most businesses have haphazard pricing.

Sometimes, you just pick a number based on how you "feel" about it. The problem is that your audience might not "feel" the same. No matter how intuitive, you are still a human being, with human biases. Pricing from a shoot-from-the-hip kind of way is not wise business practice.

Or, you might blindly trust a business/marketing expert who says that you should "<u>charge what you're worth</u>" and always go for premium pricing.

Or, you might just go with whatever your <u>niche mates</u> are charging.

In this post, I'll share a more thoughtful process to arrive at a price that feels right to you and is grounded in reality. I call it authentic pricing.

The aim is to arrive at a price where your ideal client says "That's a great deal!" ...and a price which you genuinely feel in integrity about.

1. Your Cost (of Living)

One important factor is to look at the cost of running your business.

First of all, are there any costs that are directly associated with the product, service, or program that you are offering? For example, if it's an event, what are the event's costs to you? If it's a product, what are its manufacturing costs? If it's a service, is there software that automates some part of the delivery?

If it's simply 1:1 coaching, there might be no other direct business costs.

Also take into account the indirect costs for your business, such as various software subscriptions that power your marketing, any coaching/consulting services you're receiving, any advertising costs, etc.

The revenue from all your offerings should, eventually, *more* than pay for all your costs -- direct and indirect.

Compared to all your offerings, how much time and energy does this product/service take up? Let's say it'll take up 50% of your working time. Then perhaps the revenue from this offering should pay for 50% of your indirect costs, in addition to paying for its own direct costs.

If you're a solopreneur, another indirect cost to account for is your own cost of living: rent, healthcare, food, and hopefully some regular retirement savings.

You can, of course, charge a lower rate... if you can lower your costs! If you don't figure out what is truly enough for you, your natural human appetites will keep rising, and so will your costs.

Because I've figured out my "enough", I'm able to charge a lower business coaching rate than others at my advanced experience level. My clients think, "Wow, George Kao is a great deal for expert business coaching!" and I'm glad.

I hope you'll also give your clients that feeling of excellent value.

Of course, the perceived value of your offering also depends on what you're offering, as well as your branding/reputation. We'll touch on that later.

2. Expected Sales

How many units do you expect to sell once the marketing ramps up to an expected level?

For example, if you are doing 1:1 coaching, you might want to find out from other coaches in your niche: how many billable sessions do they typically do in an average month?

If you're starting a group program, what number of people can you reasonably expect to sign up? If you're not sure, then what's the minimum number of people you'd like, in order for the program to run?

The better you understand your audience's wants and buying behavior, the more accurately you are able to determine the *expected sales.* This is why I talk about the importance of building an audience and getting to know them, first.

Dividing **Your Cost** by the **Expected Sales** will give you the minimum per-unit price that you need to charge for this offering.

To watch a tutorial of this whole process, check out my video on calculating your minimum sustainable hourly rate: https://www.youtube.com/watch?v=o0AtwdKceHc

To access the spreadsheet, click here, then click File and Make a Copy.

3. Market Rate

What does your audience expect the price of your offering should be, based on what they already know (or can quickly research)?

For example, they might expect 1:1 coaching to be somewhere between $50—$250/hour, depending on the reputation of the coach and what issues they're coaching on.

How much your audience cares about the Market Rate (compared to your rate) is determined by <u>specificity of the offering, and the audience's trust in you.</u>

This means that the more specific your offering is, the better the audience might have an idea of what the price should be. The broader your offering, the more the audience has no idea what they should be paying, and are going to be uncomfortable buying something they're not sure about.

Trust is another big factor, or what (in marketing) is called "branding". The more they trust you (the more credibility you have with them), the more your audience doesn't care about the market rate and will just go with whatever you charge.

4. Different Tiers of Offerings

Chances are, you have potential clients who are at different levels of comfort with spending money on your type of business.

As a result, it's a good idea to have different levels of offerings:

- **DIY**—an online course or automated program that allows the client to learn and practice at their own pace. Once the course is created, it costs you very little time to manage it, so you can charge less. For examples see my DIY courses: www.GeorgeKao.com/Workshops

- **Group support**—for those who want more than DIY, but aren't ready to buy your 1:1, group support is a good option. At this level, you're providing support such as through a weekly group call, and perhaps also a private Facebook group for additional support. Priced in between the DIY and 1:1 support. As an example, see my Group Coaching program: www.GeorgeKao.com/Group

- **1:1 sessions**—this, of course, takes you more time per client than the Group offering, so it would be priced higher. An example is my 1-1 coaching: www.GeorgeKao.com/Coaching

- **1:1 with emergency support**—this might be your highest level offering, where you provide not only scheduled 1:1 sessions, but also allowing your clients to request sudden/emergency "SOS" sessions, or maybe they can text you for rapid support. You therefore need to take into account how much time and energy a typical "emergency" client might cost you, and price this tier accordingly.

Additional Tips

As you get to know your audience better, you'll be able to create an offering that is even better matched for them.

Focus on creating your offering for your ideal client/customer—the ones who will get the most out of your offering, the ones who are so interested in solving the problem or reaching the goal, that they will be less concerned about the price.

In other words, work with clients who will most value what you do. Otherwise, they (and sometimes, you) will feel bad about the price.

It's okay for non-ideal clients to go elsewhere. They're only "non-ideal" for you… they might be perfect for someone else. You may, in fact, want to have a short list of alternative providers to refer to, so that you can make yourself more available to those who love your work.

Lastly, remember this: You can always change your pricing, as you come to better understand (or change) your costs and your expected sales, and as your niche adjusts its market rate over time.

Keep aiming for pricing that feels really congruent to you—neither creating resentment nor greed—and that gets a positive reaction from your clients: "I'm so grateful for this offering, and this price!"

Share this chapter, or to comment on it, using this link:
https://www.georgekao.com/blog/pricing

Chapter 13: Twenty Ways to Improve Your Offerings

The stronger your offering, the less selling is needed.

Let's say you found a cure to cancer—one that had zero negative side effects, was proven to work, and was easy to take. Word-of-mouth will spread so quickly you would never need to "sell" it!

What follows are 20 factors that, if strengthened in your offering (your service or product) would lessen your need to promote it… and yet, people would be thrilled to buy.

As you study this list, see which factors resonate with you. Even improving just 1 or 2 factors in your offering can make a difference in whether people decide to buy from you!

1. Can your offer be described as an alternative to what the audience is already used to paying for? If you're selling something the audience has never bought or considered buying, you will have to do a lot of education (or a long journey of content) before they might eventually buy. The more your offer is understandable, something they have bought or know someone who has bought, the less you'll have educate them about why it's valuable. What

similar product or service is already selling well, and how is yours better suited for your ideal audience? Perhaps your audience has tried something else before, but they didn't love it. Why not, and how can you make yours better? Example: You are a relationship coach who offers a faster alternative to traditional psychotherapy, specifically for women who seek healthier relationships after a divorce. So you position your program as a "better" alternative—not better than all psychotherapy—but better suited for that type of woman going through that type of situation. It's an alternative to what she is already paying for or would have paid for. Because she already values psychotherapy, its alternative—your service—is in a context she understands and can quickly accept.

2. Usefulness—your service is true to what your ideal clients need and want… it solves an issue that "keeps them up at night." Not only is it something you are passionate about, it's also something that they say is useful to them. Discover this by having more conversations with your audience.

3. Urgency—the more urgent their problem, the more likely people will pay for it.

4. Diagnosis—The better you understand them, the more you can pinpoint their problem. The more you can accurately diagnose their problem, the more they will trust you. Therefore grow your ability to describe their pain, their problem, their need, not to create more distress for them, but in service of connecting to them, such that they would say, "Yes, you seem to know what I'm going through!"

5. Quickness of results—this is about efficiency and effectiveness, not hype or unhealthy shortcuts. The sooner a client can experience transformation, the more they will spread the word about you and your offering.

6. Personalization—something like an e-book or webinar has the lowest personalization because the same thing is being given to lots of people. One-to-one Counseling/Coaching/Consulting, on the other hand, has high personalization as one of its strengths, and therefore you can charge more for it.

7. Delivery speed—What benefit can you give them right after they buy, so they can begin to be comforted or helped right away?

8. Enrollment Ease—is your website easy to read, delightful to look at, or is it overwhelming and

cluttered? Are your services easy to find? Is it obvious where to sign up? Does the technology meet people where they're at?

9. Your Story—what was the struggle (in you, or in the world) that inspired you to get into this field? How did you then discover the solution? What proof have you seen that the solution works? What is your passion for spreading this solution in the world, i.e. how can this change the world?

10. Branding—memorable brand name and tagline, values, and style, communicated through text, graphics, audio, video—specifically resonating with your ideal audience.

11. Entertainment value—graphic design, audio, video, humor.

12. Service first, payment later—If you deliver a service, don't be so nervous about requiring payment up front. You can be clear, in advance, what the payments are, and when they're due… but then simply start delivering the service, and remind them about the payment when it's time. Give value before expecting value.

13. Includes bite-sized pieces so people can quickly understand the benefits of your service. Examples: a virtual intuitive who does "readings" can offer email mini-readings. A life coach can offer one curated piece of content delivered to the client once per week.

14. Placement and visibility—where is your type of service already being mentioned, or bought? Examples: as a bonus to someone else's program, service, or book; In a directory of similar services (but beware of paid directories unless they have a ROI guarantee such as Noomii's); being featured in front of an audience (e.g. through a webinar) who has already been educated about similar things. Where are people asking for recommendations of services like yours?

15. Authentic, real-world limits—rather than something that is just made up to elicit fear or greed in the audience. Example, "You are being invited to apply before I send the invitation to my audience on March 17; There are just 10 spots available so that I can serve my clients well." Another example: "I'd like to start the next group of clients on April 7 so I am offering a discount for people who sign up by April 3rd."

16. Visible First Steps—can you include, within your marketing materials, any examples of people who have taken the first few steps with you? How did it go for them? This gives the audience confidence that it's a great idea to get started with you. Another option: in your free content, can you help your audience successfully take their first few steps?

17. Clarity & specificity on whom it's for—"That's exactly me!"—or "I know someone exactly like what you're describing!" If you can describe your audience in this way, you become easily referrable. Example: "My life coach specializes in working with women who are going through a divorce, and I know you're having a tough time with your divorce with Tom right now. You should give her a call." Not referable: "You should call my life coach, she's great." Most referrals occur simply because a friend has a specific challenge and the client proactively recommends *you* as a solution.

18. Client Reviews—which is to ask your clients to honestly review your service, so those who are considering buying can know whether it's the best fit for them. Ask your clients to reply to this question: "What would you say to someone who is

considering my service?"

19. Case studies—can you offer stories demonstrating in what cases your service works well? Try to offer at least 3 stories in your marketing. As you start tracking such stories, you'll start to notice the problems you most effectively solve for clients. And specifically, for what type of client. If you focus your marketing on talking about these problems and for whom your service is best suited, your marketing will become resonant!

20. Statistics of Results—if possible, offer numbers related to your service, such as number of people you've served; satisfaction rates; and any measurable thing your clients transformed in as a result of working with you.

That's a big list! Just start by getting good at *one* thing.

Imagine a scale…

On one side are the 20 Factors and how skillfully you've implemented them in your offerings.

On the other side is the Price of your offerings.

The more you've implemented the factors, the higher your Price can be.

The less you've implemented the factors, the lower your price needs to be.

The more your scale tips toward The 20 Factors, the more people will spread the word and the less selling is needed!

Keep boosting your offerings using the list above. Just return to this list occasionally and see if you can do 1 more thing to improve your offering.

One day, your offering will be so strong that you won't have to do any more promotion—all new business will come via word of mouth.

Share this chapter, or to comment on it, using this link: https://medium.com/@georgekao/20-ways-to-improve-your-marketing-offer-9de7478bc06a

Chapter 14: Credibility Indicators for Your Services

Creating a document with your credibility indicators can greatly boost your confidence, and make it easier to improve your marketing materials.

It's a document to keep private, but you will be using parts of it publicly. Open the document whenever you write or update your marketing copy, or plan a presentation for prospective clients.

Update the document gradually, over time. It will continue to remind you of how truly useful your offerings are to your ideal audience. It will build your confidence and clarity about your business.

Use these steps...

Start a blank document on your computer, and begin by adding any of the following elements. You don't have to add everything. Just look through these following 10 factors and start anywhere:

1. Any testimonials you've gotten about your work. Sometimes that's just a nice email from someone you helped. Or social media reviews or comments you've received (that's what I prefer, and do on my site.) Or perhaps in a conversation with a client, they said something about how your service helped them. It may be easiest to record your client conversations (with their permission) and ask them how your work has helped them. And then transcribe and edit it, and ask if you can use it as a testimonial. In mentioning the client's name (if they allow it), also include any relevant identifying info that your prospective client would relate to, e.g. profession, location, any demographics like "Mom of 2 kids".

2. Any case studies e.g. what people were like before working with you; what was the process you led them through; and what their life was like afterwards, sharing the specifics of their transformation. Make each story as concise as possible—just a few paragraphs.

3. The story of your own transformation (if applicable)

The **Struggle** that you experienced—yours or someone else's—that made you want to look for a solution. This helps you connect more with the audience—they'll see that you're just a human being like they are.

The story of how you came across your **Solution** (mountaintop experience; wise mentor; training or certification you received; your own experiments and life learning.)

The **Proof** that the solution really works—in your life and/or someone else's

The **Passion** you have for offering the solution to the world…that it's not (just) about the money, but about the service/impact/legacy.

4. Anywhere you or your work has been featured: articles, guest blog posts, radio shows/podcasts, telesummits, awards you've won, etc.

Start collecting links of web pages, and posts, that feature you.

A short list of links to webpages that have mentioned you is especially useful to include when reaching out to prospective promotional partners or prospective clients. It's proof that others are talking about you, and what they're saying.

These links could be as simple as a public Facebook post that a fan/friend has written about your work. (To get the link to a particular facebook post, click the timestamp of that post to get the URL.)

5. Statistics about your work. For example:

- Years of studying your topic (or if you prefer, how many hundreds or thousands of hours).

- The approximate number of people you've helped with your work over the years—volunteer or paid.

- Satisfaction rates of clients you've served. (e.g. "80% of my clients say they experience this kind of transformation.")

- Approximately how many people you've spoken in front of or how many speeches/webinars/videos you've given about your work.

- The number of tools (exercises, templates, processes, assignments) you are able to use with your clients.

- Any other number you can put to your work. Get creative with how you express "numbers" in showing credibility about your work.

6. Relevant degrees, trainings, coursework, or certifications.

7. Relevant groups or associations you're a part of.

8. Any endorsements about you or your work from anyone famous.

"Famous" means anyone your audience would have heard of. This might be industry-specific.

9. Rave reviews about any product/book/teleseminar/course you've created.

10. Famous clients you've worked with that you are able to mention.

When in doubt, check with your clients first, before naming them in any marketing communications.

There may be other credibility indicators you can come up with. If so, add them to your document!

Remember: any *one* of the above can make you appear credible, if the indicator is relevant to the person or audience you're talking to.

This document that you create will continually remind you of the credibility and impact of your work, and will strengthen your confidence to do your outreach and marketing.

Anytime you are writing marketing copy for your website, or communicating with a prospective client, this document can serve as a resource.

Keep adding to this document, and rearranging it so the most impressive indicators are in the beginning.

Share this chapter, or to comment on it, using this link: https://medium.com/@georgekao/template-credibility-indicators-for-your-services-8cde81ca8f0f

Section 3:

Ideas for Authentic Outreach

Chapter 15: How to Get Clients as an Authentic Business

This chapter is written especially for those of you who are selling something unique, possibly offering a service or product that has been rarely seen.

This means that people aren't used to buying your product, and it won't be as easy to market, compared to a mainstream service or commodity product.

How then can you actually get clients, and have it occur on a consistent basis? In this chapter I'll describe 4 important pieces to the puzzle.

Ask yourself which of the following are missing in your business, and work to fill those gaps, one by one…

Trust

Before anyone will hire you or buy from you, they need to have enough trust in your business.

Trust with someone (or an audience) can be built in various ways:

- You've <u>created content</u> that is relevant to them. It's helpful, or inspiring, or deeply meaningful to them.
- You've shown yourself as <u>authentic in your content or your marketing</u>. They feel you're being honest and true to who you are.
- You've been <u>showing up consistently in your content</u>, or email newsletters.
- Your Consistency = Your Reliability, in your audience's mind.
- You've gotten <u>endorsements</u> (positive mentions, testimonials, recommendations, positive reviews) from people or sources that they trust. This requires you to do some networking, perhaps gifting some of your services to influencers who have an audience you want to reach.
- Your visual branding looks trustworthy to them. This will depend on what other brands they trust, and how your branding measures up to what they're used to seeing.

You don't need to have all of the above.

Excellence in **any one of the above** can build enough trust to make enough sales. Or you can aim to be decent in several of these.

For example, I've practiced becoming skillful in creating content consistently. I've collected client testimonials. Yet, when it comes to visual branding, I'm more or less ignoring it… however, I still have more than enough clients.

Which one or two of the above factors can you improve most easily, to build trust with your audience? There's no one "right" answer here except what you can become excellent at. Focus your efforts for better results.

Alignment

You are offering a product or service that is aligned with what they are used to buying or can imagine themselves buying.

This sounds obvious, but it's hard to do, especially if you're selling a unique transformational service. (For example, most people aren't used to buying "coaching" or "mentoring" or "healing" services yet.)

How do you break through when you're offering a new service that people aren't used to buying?

Here are some ideas:

- Offer your expertise in a format that many people (in your audience) are used to buying. Common examples are Books, eBooks, Audiobooks, and Online Courses. Then, once they have a positive experience of buying one of these things from you, they're more likely to buy other things from you, that they hadn't previously considered, e.g. Coaching, Healing, Mentoring or a Group Program. It can be enlightening for you to have conversations (or use a survey) with your audience to find out what they have bought, that is related to your area of expertise.

- Describe what you do, in your content and marketing, in ways that help your ideal clients envision themselves experiencing your service. For example, tell stories in your content about your work with your clients (keep those clients anonymous, unless they've given you permission). Or interview your happy and willing clients to share their story of working with you. I have a video series like this that I call <u>Client Lessons</u>.

- Offer samples of what you do. You can let your audience/network know that you are giving away a limited number of free 1–1 sessions. Or record a Zoom call with you and a willing client (or supportive friend) where you are actually doing your service for that person, and if you have their permission, share that video or audio in your content and marketing, so that others can get a taste of what it's like to work with you.

- Offer a live (in person or online) group experience that is free or low cost, where you are demonstrating your expertise, giving them an experience they'll find useful or be delighted by. An example is Ruth Toledo Altschuler, a Flower Essence Practitioner who offers [free online Healing Circle experiences](). An example of a low-cost experience is [my online workshops]().

- Encourage your existing clients to refer you to their friends. There are many ways to do this. One example: Give your happy clients a Gift Certificate that they can hand to their friends. Everyone wins: your happy clients enjoy sharing a deal for a service they believe in; their friends who need your service get to try it out; and you get new clients.

- If you don't have any clients yet, or not enough clients to be able to easily do the above actions, then try this: Ask the people you know if they are willing to try out your service, without charge, so that you can develop some case studies. Even if they would prefer to be anonymous, you can describe the case studies in your content and marketing, in a way that keeps their privacy.

You can get clients by doing any one of the above enough to become excellent at it. Try different ways. Then commit to doing one or more of the above consistently.

Specificity

Imagine if I offered you this deal:

Just pay me $1,000 and we'll spend a few hours together. We'll talk about whatever you want in your business!

You're not likely to take me up on that. (At least, I hope you aren't that easily sold!)

If I change it to something much more specific, it becomes more effective:

With 2 billion active users on Facebook, a lot of your ideal clients are on that platform, most of them daily. For $1,000 I will do 1–1 coaching with you during a 3-month period to customize a highly effective monthly plan for your Facebook Marketing that fits your business and style. Once the plan is created, you'll be able to keep implementing the plan, month after month, to grow your ideal audience by 10x–100x. You'll be using Facebook more effectively than the vast majority of business owners.

(This is something I actually do with clients.)

Another example, in a different field:

Hire me as your relationship coach. I will help you find more love in your relationship.

So many people are essentially marketing their business in vague ways like this.

Something more specific would be more effective:

Let's start with 3 sessions of coaching, where we will dive into questions that reveal the big picture of your relationship, as well as the roots of what is holding you back as a couple. You and I will then decide the top 3 easily doable actions that will increase joyful excitement, intimacy, and abiding trust into your relationship.

Another example:

My mentorship will get you to the next level of your career. (Too broad.)

More specificity, more effectiveness:

My clients are unhappy at work because they can't get their ideas heard and implemented in the company. When you do 6 months of mentorship with me, I will work with you to map out the specific levers of change in your company (people, meetings, projects, and scripts) that will get your best 3 ideas considered by the executive team and have at least 1 of your ideas implemented, with credit to you.

(I'm neither a relationship coach nor a career/executive coach, so the above examples can probably be made more relevant to actual clients, if that is your field of expertise.)

Also, in the examples above, I mentioned "3 sessions" or "6 months"—remember that you can always extend your work with clients, if the initial sessions are useful to them.

I hope the idea is clear: bring more specificity into your marketing, and it will tend to increase its effectiveness.

Invitations

I find that many business owners I work with (perhaps you as well) seem to be having this problem: you aren't letting your audience know, often enough, what it is that you do, and how they can work with you!

If your audience doesn't know about your offering, or hasn't seen it lately, you're making it hard for them to say Yes to hiring you.

If you don't invite them to the party, why would they feel welcome? How do you know?
Once you are doing the above—building trust, finding alignment, being specific—then I encourage you to get into a rhythm of inviting your audience to your offerings on a regular basis.

Ways to invite:

- Include a mention of your offering(s) in your regular (monthly or weekly) email newsletter. To see how I do this, <u>subscribe to my newsletter</u>.

- Have a rhythm of posting about your offering(s) on your Facebook business page. You can see my FB business page <u>here</u>.

- Have a rhythm of personally contacting your biggest supporters and past clients and referral sources. (See the next chapter.) For example, if you have 50 people you want to personally keep in touch with every 3 months, it would only require you to touch base with 4 people per week. Very doable. You'll be better at keeping in touch with people than the vast majority of business owners!

Do you have questions about any of the above? Let me know by commenting here.

The most important thing is to get started. Re-read this chapter, and see what pieces of the puzzle you're missing, and get working on it.

Remind yourself of how helpful your service will be to your ideal client, if only they trusted you enough, and understood your service enough, to say Yes.

Share this chapter, or to comment on it, using this link:
https://www.georgekao.com/blog/gettingclients

Chapter 16: Need Clients ASAP? The Power of Personal Outreach

Your own network often forget what exactly you do for work.

So if you aren't keeping in touch, how will they remember to refer you new clients?

Out of the hundreds of entrepreneurs and service providers I have personally coached, I can count on one hand (i.e. very few!) the number of people who, before they started working with me, were consistently and personally keeping in touch with their network about what they do.

Personal outreach is a higher quality of contact than just seeing your posts on social media, and it's what can get you clients faster.

Here's the simple method:

Personally reach out to 50 individuals, with a message customized for each person.

It's about being a blessing to others... to be of genuine usefulness to them or to their friends.

Here are 5 categories of people to reach out to, and what you might say to them...

1. Supportive Friends

Who are the friends that are most supportive of your business?

To get some ideas:
- Whom have you been texting?
- Look at your email "sent" folder -- those you've emailed recently.
- Open your phone's "history" -- whom have you called in the past few months?
- Look at your list of Facebook friends -- which of them would likely love to help you, if only they knew how?

Some thoughts of what to say in your message to them...

1. I would love your help with a little bit of outreach, to fill some client openings.
2. I love what I do, and I'm great at helping _____ [this type of person]_____.
3. Here are a few of the most important problems that my service helps people to solve... [list them in bullet points]

4. Here's what a few of my clients have said... [give 2-3 short testimonials]
5. Do you have friends who could use this kind of help?
6. If so, I'd be happy to sit down with them for [a free 1-hour consultation] to figure out their needs, see how I can help them.
7. Let me know if you have any questions I can answer, to make it easier for you to think of whom would be ideal to introduce to me.
8. Here's the simplest way to introduce them to me (e.g. send them an email and CC me, and I'll take it from there.)
9. I'll take great care of the people you send me!

As you look at these ideas, be sure to write the message in *your* voice and a way that feels natural to the particular relationship, to the person you're reaching out to. This is where a lot of people trip up -- they just follow a template and ignore the relationship that is there. It's best that you be natural and true to that friendship. Be real, not salesy.

The only exception is your email newsletter. When someone subscribes to that, they are expecting the same message sent to all your subscribers.

But when you are personally reaching out to someone, not via an email newsletter, it is more respectful to customize the message as much as possible, given the relationship you have with them.

Write from the heart, and take into account what you understand about them.

---

2. Your Fans:

- People who have emailed you inquiries in the past
- Your email newsletters' top openers
- Private/inbox messages on your FB Business Page
- Commenters on your Facebook posts
- Those who engage with (like or comment on) your LinkedIn posts
- Engagers in your other relevant social media posts (on Insta, Twitter, etc.)

If people are already engaging with you in any of the above, then they are possibly open to your offerings.

Use a similar template, as above, to contact them.

3. Your Former Clients

Given the principles as above (i.e. use your own voice, not this exact template, and customize it for the person), here is the gist of what to communicate:

1. How's it going with [the issue you worked with them on]?
2. Here's a piece of content I thought you might find helpful for that issue.... [give link to one of your articles/videos, or someone else's content that you found helpful.]
3. I've got availability in my business right now. If you'd like to schedule something, here's the link... (or I've got an upcoming event and thought of you... here's the link.)
4. Let me know if I can answer any questions!
5. Either way, I'd love to hear how you are doing. Reply when you have a moment!

---

4. Your Colleagues

For this activity, I define a "colleague" as someone you don't know as well as a "supportive friend", but someone you feel resonant with, and has a network/clientele of people similar to your ideal clients.

Where are your colleagues? Find them in:

- <u>your list of Facebook friends</u>
- <u>the Facebook Groups you're in</u>
- <u>your LinkedIn contacts</u>

1. First, go to their Facebook profile, and scroll down to see what they've been posting lately. Keep scrolling until you find something that you personally resonate with. It could be a life event of theirs that you want to say something about. Or some help they asked for. Or some topic they posted on, that you have an opinion about.

2. Send them a Facebook Private Message:

- Start by saying something supportive, based on what you saw from their recent postings.

- Say that you'd like to reconnect with them, and see how you might support each other's businesses. For example, you could give feedback on each other's websites or services. Or you could talk about whether there might be any referral possibilities to one another.

5. Influencers (think of them as future colleagues!)

These are people you don't know yet, who have an audience of your ideal clients, and who doesn't do exactly what you do. It would make sense for them to share your stuff, if they trusted you and your offerings.

Reach out to them. They won't have the opportunity to support you, and for you to support them and their audience... unless you give them that opportunity.

One way is to go to LinkedIn Groups and use the search function at the top of that page, to find a general topic that is similar to what you provide, e.g. someone who does Energy Healing might search "Spirituality" on LinkedIn. Then, you'll see groups and how many members per group. The owners of those LinkedIn groups are able to send an email announcement to about 80% of their members... so essentially you can see from the search results how big their email audience is.

Click on the group then click on the Owner's linkedin profile. Then find their website (or Google them) and find their email address.

When you look at their LinkedIn profile, if you have a mutual connection that might be willing to introduce the two of you, do it that way. Otherwise, sending an email directly to them is fine, or send a private message to them on Facebook:

1. Give them genuine praise for the group they've built / their online presence.
2. Mention that they seem like someone who might be open to collaboration.
3. Invite them to reply if they're open to exploring possible ways to support each other. Or directly give them a link to schedule a "get to know you" 15-30 minute call with you.

When they reply back, you might ask them:

Are you open to receiving commissions, if there is something I can offer that your audience would love?

Be open to offering your program or service (e.g. 1 or 2 sessions) to them for free, to get a taste of what you do.

Some encouragement...

What's perhaps the only real thing that is holding you back from this activity? Your own fear. And, you probably have your own mental/emotional/energy tools to resolve this fear.

Or, reach out to a friend, colleague, or coach to have them apply their tools on your hesitations, doubts, fears.

Remove your fear... and replace it with love.

By lovingly taking the actions above, you'll gain new clients soon.

Remember: in the beginning of your business, before you have a large enough audience who loves your content and naturally shares it forward, you need to do more personal outreach.

Keep contacting different people, in a service-oriented way, until someone says Yes. Always make it a custom message, to respect that person and what you know about them.

And keep updating the way you do this, as you experiment and learn.

Some business gurus like Gary Vaynerchuk encourage us to reach out to 1,000 people and maybe expect 10 to say Yes. That may be too extreme... so I'm asking you to just reach out to 50 or 100 for now... and if you follow my suggestions above, you will likely get new clients.

The best way of doing all this is with no expectations or requirements from any specific person that you're reaching out to. Do it from a sense of service for them.

Remember that whenever it's the right fit, you are a blessing to them.

You won't know until you try!

Share this chapter, or to comment on it, using this link:
https://www.georgekao.com/blog/clientsasap

Chapter 17: Three Circles of Outreach

You don't need to enroll the world. There is a limited number of clients you can serve **well** at any given time. Clarify how many that is for you. Remember that number. See how valuable, therefore, **each** of those client spots are.

Most service providers are assuming that they need to be afraid of people *not* saying Yes to them.

I recommend turning that thought around. Do you realize that you have to say **Yes** to a new client before they are *allowed* into your energetic/mental space, before they are allowed to use your services?

The time in your business when you are launching, or whenever you are open to new clients, is the time that you get to *choose and allow* just the right people to be able to say Yes to your business.

I think about 3 circles of outreach to allow in, starting with the inner circle, those closest to you.

Your INNER Circle

This is comprised of your current clients, previous clients, potential clients (those who have inquired with you), your closest friends and colleagues, and your biggest fans.

Current Clients: Those who are getting good results, or are likely to get good results if they keep working with you. During your launch or enrollment period, it would make sense to give them first dibs on keeping the spots they already have with you, i.e. to renew your joint commitment to working with each other. You can also invite them to let a few of their right contacts know, those who can really benefit from your service.

Previous Clients: Those who had good results with your products/services, and might want to continue.

Prospective Clients: Those who expressed interest in working with you. They had an exploratory call with you, or otherwise inquired about your services, but the timing hadn't been right yet. Reach out now, as the timing may be better. Give them the chance to say Yes before you move onto the "Middle" circle.

Closest Friends & Colleagues: Especially those who have expressed interest in your services, or have been supportive of you. Let them know that you are now enrolling new clients, and that if they have a friend or colleague who could benefit from your services (briefly describe how) that you will be honored to take great care of them.

Any other big fans who aren't already in your INNER circle. Ideally, individually reach out to them to give the opportunity.

As you reach out to all the people above, **gently mention a due date** of 1-2 weeks to respond, letting them know that you would prefer to save a spot for them (or their recommended referrals), before you offer the same opportunity to your wider network. Ask them to let you know by [Exact Date] if possible. Then, 1-2 days before the date, send them a **reminder** about this opportunity.

You can either reach out to these people one-to-one... (better if you have the time and energy) or, you can simply send a BCC email (blind-carbon-copy) them all with the purpose of not giving any one person pressure, but wanting to make sure they all know. Also, let them know that you will be reminding them with another email in 1 week (or whatever timing makes sense). Just be sure that whomever you choose to BCC would likely welcome your email.

Your MIDDLE Circle

Promotional Partners: If you've had people promote/share your content or services in the past, consider reaching out to them now about this launch.

Your middle circle also contains:
- **Your social media audience**, whichever platforms you use (e.g. Facebook, Instagram, Twitter, Linkedin, etc.)
- Send this opportunity to **your email subscribers**
- If you have a **blog or podcast**, mention it or do a special piece of content about your offering.

Your OUTER Circle

If the inner and middle circles aren't enough to fill your clientele, then it's time to move into the outer circle, which is unlimited.

This includes promotional partners (influencers) you *don't* already know. Be sure to access the Bonus Materials for 3 additional chapters on how (and why) to reach out to promotional partners. Get the bonus materials by filling out the survey for this book: www.GeorgeKao.com/BookSurvey

Your outer circle may also include:

- **Facebook Ads and Google Ads**, if you have a budget to experiment with. To learn how to do paid advertising, check out my courses: www.GeorgeKao.com/workshops
- Individually reaching out via LinkedIn to **prospective clients** who don't yet know you. The key is to keep remembering that you are coming from a place of service, seeking to align to their wants and needs, rather than trying to persuade or "get" them to do something.

For each of your launches (focused times in your business when you are filling client spots), keep coming back to these circles.

Remember that you are simply giving each circle a chance (1-2 weeks) to enroll or refer, before you move onto the next circle.

If however your enrollment isn't working at all, you will need to revisit your Offer, and optimize it further. See the chapters 9-14 for that help.

Share this chapter, or to comment on it, using this link:
https://www.facebook.com/GeorgeKaoCommunity/posts/10154999590549867/

Chapter 18: Complimentary Call Launch

A few times a year, when you are needing to fill your client spots, consider doing a "complimentary call launch."

This type of launch is where you offer a large number of such calls in a short time period e.g. 1-4 weeks. (You can, of course, weave this into your "3 circles" launch, as mentioned in the previous chapter.)

"Complimentary calls" are also known as: discovery calls, exploratory sessions, clarity calls, or strategy sessions.

Here is a basic email template:

"From September 15-30, I am focused on giving complimentary coaching sessions to as many people as I can. During these sessions, I will help you [create some small, real transformation / get some important clarity on my area of expertise -- be sure to describe it.] The people that get the most out of these sessions are [describe your ideal client.] If that sounds like you, I encourage you to request a session here [give link to your session request page.] If that describes a friend or colleague, feel free to forward this email to them!"

(Carefully read and customize the above template for your own business!)

Let's say you send this email on September 1. Then, you send a reminder email on Sept 10, then finally another reminder on Sept 20.

A good example of this is from Nav Scheie:
https://www.facebook.com/nav.scheie/posts/10157332465270290

Send your invitation to your email list subscribers, to your friends, colleagues, clients, past clients, and post on all social media channels you're active in.

Before you do a Complimentary Call Launch, you may want to first get feedback about your free call. I share how to do that here:
https://www.facebook.com/GeorgeKaoCommunity/posts/10154819169499867/

You can comment on this chapter here:
https://www.facebook.com/GeorgeKaoCommunity/posts/10154896093134867/

Chapter 19: How *Not* to Have a Sales Conversation

Think back to the last time you experienced a sales conversation.

Were you in the process of buying something? Or maybe you were on the selling side.

When it's done well, a sales conversation can give both parties a sense of joyful connection, genuine helping, and an expression of authentic enthusiasm.

Unfortunately, a sales conversations can also feel awkward, anxious, or even manipulative. It can also create defensiveness in the seller and therefore suspiciousness on the buyer's side.

Here's an experience I actually had when I was a potential client for someone else. I found a coaching program that I was interested in, to help me improve my own coaching skills. I filled out the application. The day came when I got to talk with the seller.

I was hoping that the conversation would generate a genuine feeling of connection and helping.

Instead, after two minutes of pleasantries, his first question was:

"So... what's your insecurity about your coaching?" (Literally what he said.)

I've studied traditional sales methods a bit, and I could imagine what this guy was doing -- having me feel my FUD (fear, uncertainty, and doubt) so that he can insert his solution, as the way out of my pain.

I paused and said "um...", kind of surprised he would be so brazen about trying to increase my feelings of insecurity.

He noticed my pause... and immediately asked this question:

"What makes you interested in the program?"

Before I could answer, he said...

"Is it [benefit A], [benefit B], or [benefit C]?"

There it is. Traditional sales: Stoke the prospect's fear, uncertainty, or doubt, and then entice them with the benefits of your solution.

We're only a few minutes into the conversation, and already it felt awkward. Especially because I could see the sales techniques he was employing on me. Why would he do this? It seemed like he has practiced the techniques so much, that he's simply on autopilot, not truly connected to the moment.

Instead of seeking a genuine connection, he was just trying to make the sale.

I would've given him the benefit of the doubt if he was a newbie marketer who was simply parroting his sales coach. But this is no newbie -- this guy himself actually has another program that **teaches** sales. I was expecting him to be more savvy at this.

Truly savvy salespeople never make you feel like you're being sold.

I hope you become a savvy salesperson, but *not due to* techniques or scripts.

My recommendation is to get rid of the "sales" mindset, and instead, connect from the heart, with an authentic mindset of caring and service, and *not be concerned* with whether they buy in that conversation… or ever.

In fact, don't keep looking for a "bridge" in the conversation, to finally be able to talk about what you want to sell.

The framework I'm about to share with you will tend to work well, especially for building loyal long-term relationships with clients and referral sources. The problem is, if you turn my framework into a technique or script, it starts to feel fake. So the key is to look past the technique, to the heart of the ideas, and practice embodying those values.

Here's the simple framework:

Focus 80% of your conversation time on connecting with where they're at, and caring genuinely about what they're going through. They're *already* experiencing fear, uncertainty, and doubt in their life. You don't need to rub it in.

If you genuinely connect with them and make them feel safe, they will naturally start to talk about the issues you can help with. And then, being in a heartset of service, you will naturally try to help with a bit of advice.

Perhaps you might start with mirroring back what you heard, in your words, to see if you understood them. Then you might go into some diagnosis, to help them understand some of the root of their symptoms, problems, or challenges, from your expertise.

These are not so much *sales* techniques (connection, safety, mirroring, diagnosis, advice) as they are techniques of *being a good friend.*

In other words, in these conversations, focus 80% of the time on simply being a helpful person. For the final 20% of the time (about 5 minutes before the end of a 30 minute conversation), start to complete the meeting with this simple question:

"Looks like our time is about up… do you happen to have any questions about how I work with clients [or about the program or about the product]?"

(Ask that question in your own style.)

And then pause. If they are indeed interested, they will ask you questions.

Then simply answer their questions, once again being in a mindset of caring and service, not trying to "convert" the sale.

Here's an important caveat -- I am assuming that this is an exploratory conversation they requested because they are already interested in your services.

If you are instead in a conversation where the person is *unaware* of your services, or you're not sure they're interested, then focus *100% of the time* on being a friend.

Only when it's *them pursuing you* do I recommend taking the final 20% of the conversation to focus on your business, by asking the question above (in your own style).

So let's back up a bit here -- how do you get others to pursue your services and request an exploratory conversation?

My favorite way is through authentic content marketing. This is why I talk so much about it. Become a legend (or at least, trusted by your audience) through your content, and you'll have plenty of ideal clients pursuing you. This requires you to clarify your core message, develop your voice, and grow your ability to engage online, and what's the best way to do that? Get started, get consistent, and get feedback. You will definitely get clearer and better over time.

Let me complete the story that began this chapter. As we neared the end of the awkward conversation, where he spent much of the time talking about the superiority of his method, and how great his 8-week group program was, and how it's "only $3,000... I know, people say I should charge more..." (literally what he said), I said that I had to get going.

He ended the conversation by saying: "Oh, there's just one more thing... you had mentioned earlier that you charge much less than most of your peers and that you're fine with it... I think there's something there to explore? We can have another conversation where we dig into this important issue..." he said, in a tone suggesting that there was something *wrong* with what I was doing. But it's not an "issue" for me. I'm happy with what I charge. I didn't ask for his help here.

He was implementing the technique of *always leaving the client hanging a bit in doubt or fear,* so they would look forward to having that open loop *resolved* in the next conversation.

This experienced coach could've gotten a new friend in me, a new advocate, and maybe even a new client. Instead? Well... I'm grateful he inspired this chapter!

I hope that by reading this, you'll become a bit more savvy and notice these sly sales techniques, so that you can exit those conversations quickly... and be sure not to emulate them in your own work as well.

The bottom line:

Make your sales conversations about connecting & caring, rather than scripts and techniques.

And, if you feel like trying to follow my 80/20 formula above feels like a technique, then just ignore this, and simply remember one thing:

Be a friend.

**Check out the companion video for this chapter:
www.bit.ly/asbookvid19**

Chapter 20: More About Authentic Sales Conversations

Here's the framework for a Typical Sales Conversation:

1. Help them connect to their pain again, the frustration, the block, the symptoms that made them seek out a solution. Ask questions or tell stories to get them to really feel the pain and how bad it would be to stay there. (Ideally, they should feel some desperation.)

2. We're also supposed to get them to dream about what's possible, the ideal life they could have, if that pain weren't there, if they could achieve their goal successfully, how pleasurable and awesome it would be.

3. Finally, we're supposed to show them that we (our services program / product) are the bridge from the current pain to the future ideal … or our services are a "boat" that takes them from "pain island" to "pleasure island".

4. We overcome any objections they might have to signing up. Make sure to have a polished and persuasive answer to any "but what about…?" questions they might have about working with us.

5. We interject some scarcity (time limit to signing up while spaces are available, or to take advantage of a dramatic discount, or an amazing bonus) to get them to make a decision on that call if possible, or within 48 hours.

Power Over Others

In short, we are taught to skillfully manipulate the prospect's emotions and frame of mind, until they are like putty in our hands, to be shaped how we will.

This is what it means to have psychological/emotional power over someone.
This is profitable, the sales experts tell us, because now they will do what we say: spend the money we ask them to spend, and take the actions we recommend... all in service to "make their life better."

My belief is that to really make someone's life better, we should let them exercise choice and power in their life as much as possible... including making mistakes.

I'm assuming we're working with adults here. Allow them to make any decisions—especially about money and commitment—with as little pressure as possible.

Let it be something they're genuinely excited by. Let them pursue you, rather than you having to persuade them.

Be honest and transparent about what results can be expected. Search within yourself and eliminate any manipulation you feel tempted by.

This is what Authentic Sales is about.

"Heart-Based" or "Conscious" Sales Strategies?

The traditional sales method I described above is currently being dressed up by the modern "conscious" or "heart-based" business coaches who say:

"Using the pain-to-pleasure-island method, we are empowering them to make an 'investment' in themselves… we need to use techniques that get them to shed their RESISTANCE, to take INSTANT action… we manipulate them purposefully, to help them better their life."

"Of course, we don't want to mention that the majority of people who 'made an investment in their life' with our program, did not achieve the results we promise in our marketing… because it's really up to them… it's not *our* fault if it didn't work for *them*."

I hope you can now see through their rationalizations. These marketers are making money hand-over-fist by "helping" people make "an investment in their life". I've lost count of how many clients have spent tens of thousands of dollars on such programs, before they came to me.

Diagnosis & Empathy vs. Manipulation & Persuasion

The problem here is not actually with the pain/pleasure island framework.

It's about correctly naming their symptoms, so that you can diagnose the *cause* of those symptoms. This way, they can see that you can actually help them.

It's about empathy.

The problem arises when we try to use the pain/pleasure island as a tool to *manipulate* their emotions (experiencing low and high feelings) so that they buy from us.

Truth: They already know their pain. You don't need to rub it in.

You can, however, take a few moments to make sure you actually do *understand* their pain, not as part of an agenda to sell them, but from a spirit of connection and helping.

Here's an alternative sales conversation that can feel more authentic...

Authentic Sales Conversation

1. **CONNECT** with that person genuinely—as a possible future friend—to discover what it is they are really needing and wanting at this time, to see if it honestly makes sense for your business to help them at this stage. Or, is it better for you to refer them onward to another trusted provider or resource that can better help them?

Be in service, but don't underestimate the value of what you can bring to their life. If they are interested to work with you, and you believe you actually can help, then allow them to say yes. Try not to oversell (but don't undersell either) what you truly believe you can do to help them.

2. **ASK**. Prioritize asking questions rather than monologuing about your qualities and credibility.

What are their goals or vision? (As related to your area of expertise.)

Where or how are they challenged now, in the realm of things you do with clients?

What have they tried, and why didn't it work?

3. **SERVE** them in that initial conversation. Give them a sample of what you do with clients. Observe how open they

are to your efforts. Are they eager for your help? If so, they will likely be open to your help, going forward. Or are they reluctant or giving you objections? You are interviewing them, as much as they are getting to know you.

Be careful not to overwhelm them, because that wouldn't help, but also don't be holding back any idea or process that you believe would really help them in that moment.

Learning this balance takes practice. Start with your next conversation.

4. **INVITE**. 5 minutes before the end of the call, try saying: "So, do you have any questions about how I work with clients?" Ask this question only if you truly feel that your service would be a great next step for them.

If they respond eagerly, then you can simply answer their questions and talk about how to start working with you.

If however you feel that another provider or resource would honestly be the best next step or a better fit for their style, ask if they would like you to refer them onto another resource. If they insist on working with you, and you don't feel your service is the best fit at this time, you can recommend a DIY product of yours, or add them to your waiting list.

If they give you a lackluster response to this question, then they are usually not ready to work with you. You can complete the conversation. You'll have learned a bit more about who is an ideal client vs. who isn't, and perhaps you will have helped that person whether or not they ever become a client.

Timing: In my exploratory conversations, I basically spend about 5 minutes in the Connect stage, 5-10 minutes Asking questions, 10-15 minutes on Serving them, and the final 5 minutes on the Invite, as mentioned above.

Does this framework feel more authentic and service-oriented to you? Go ahead and try it.

You will be creating potential client relationships in an honest, supportive way. It will feel great to you and them. Good word will spread about your business.

By contrast, if you use the traditional sales method, you are immediately starting the relationship from a place of emotional manipulation and creating a power-over-them dynamic. Then you'll feel like you have to keep up that front as you continue working with them.

Rather than the typical spirit of Performing and Persuading in a sales conversation, let's switch to a deeper intention of Connection and Service.

I wish for you genuine, truly supportive conversations and relationships with clients going forward.

Share this chapter, or to comment on it, using this link:
https://medium.com/@georgekao/authentic-sales-conversations-1a4a8145ea4e

Chapter 21: When Not Enough People are Signing Up

You love helping people with your skills and passion.

You've been trying to sell your services. But what if not enough people are buying?

Let's take a look at the 3 reasons why people might not be buying from you and some solutions you might want to implement.

Audience

Perhaps you are not yet talking to enough people who are likely to buy your services.

You might be interacting a lot with people who have never bought or don't usually spend money on services like yours.

For example, if you are selling relationship counseling services and your audience hasn't even bought therapy (mainstream alternative to what you offer), it will be a long road before they decide to spend money on your services.

You can always change audiences.

There are 2 ways to do this:

1. Successful Niche Mates.

Network until you find a successful <u>niche mate</u> who already has an audience that is buying this type of service.

(a) If they provide a service that is the same as what you sell, you can contact them about maybe referring overflow clients to you, so you can take good care of the people that they aren't able to.

(b) Or, if they don't sell exactly your type of service, maybe they would be happy to share your service as a complementary offering to what they sell. They might be happy to do this on a commission basis, or a cross-promotion (i.e. you also recommend clients to them).

2. Paid Advertising.

Advertise your content (and eventually, your services) to the audiences that are more likely to buy.

For example, you can do this using Facebook Ads, by defining an advertising audience of people who are of a certain demographic, and are interested in the issues you help people with, or who follow famous authors, organizations, or companies who recommend (or sell) your type of service.

If you're interested, I have an <u>online course that teaches Facebook Advertising step by step</u>.

With paid advertising, you might still need to offer a lower-price front-end product (such as a short online course) to ease them into buying from you. We'll talk about that next.

Pricing

Your audience might think that your fees are too high.

Don't be swayed by the high-priced business coaches who tell you to <u>"charge what you're worth."</u> ...because you're worth an infinite amount of money. You are priceless, and so are your services.

Maybe what you are offering your audience right now is priced higher than what they want to pay at this moment. It's not that they "can't afford it" (even if they tell you that) but often, it's because they haven't budgeted to spend their money with your type of service.

You'll know this if you're talking to a prospective client on the phone, and you present your price, and they are surprised by how much it is... "sticker shock."

If they've never spent money with you before, then they need to be eased into it, rather than asked to jump off a cliff with your high-priced offer. This is especially true if they have rarely (or never) spent that kind of money on this type of service before.

There are a couple of solutions:

1. Low-Price Offer.

Offer something lower price on the "front end" (i.e. what can be found via your website and social media).

This might be a $25 online workshop, or a $10 book, or a $50 online course.

Then, for those who buy your low-price offer, you can then offer a mid-price option to work further with you, e.g. a $100 4-week program, or a $100/month group program, or a $300 for one month of 2 private sessions with you.

Then after that, to those who bought the mid-priced offer, you can see if offering your higher-priced services and packages would feel appropriate.

2. Joint Venture with a Niche Mate.

Joint Venture (JV) in this context means simply connecting with a Niche Mate about possibly promoting your low-price offer to their audience, and sharing commissions (e.g. 50%) with them.

If they have an audience, the fact that they're a niche mate means that their audience would likely find your offerings beneficial. It can be a win-win-win: Your niche mate receives commissions from you (and thanks from their audience for introducing you), their audience wins by having the benefit of your offering, and you win by having new potential clients.

3. Build Your Credibility.

The more credibility you have in the minds of your audience, the more likely they'll buy from you, and the more they'll be willing to pay.

Let's think together about this.

Credibility

Even though your audience may need the help, they may not be sure that you can really help them.

Think about Brene Brown, or Gary Vaynerchuk, or _____ fill in the blank for someone you admire in your field.

Imagine that they offered you a 1-1 private session.

Because they have enormous credibility in your mind, you might be happy to pay $1,000 for a private hour with them, fully focused on you. (Some people would pay much more for that opportunity!)

And yet, people think that your $100/hour (or whatever you charge) is too high a price?

That's because they don't believe you have enough credibility.

Here are some solutions:

1. Client Case Studies.

Share your client case studies more often on your social media, as well as in your email newsletter.

To get those case studies, you may need to offer your service at a much lower price, or for free, in exchange for being able to use someone's story as a case study. Offer this to people you believe can really benefit from what you do.

2. Influencer Case Studies.

The most impactful kind of case study is from someone who has an audience you would love to reach. Which blogger, FB Page owner, Instagram influencer, video channel, or popular podcast host, would likely enjoy your services, and have an audience that needs it?

If you are able to network your way to being in touch with them, and offer them your service in exchange for a testimonial (or simply, feedback), that could be a big opportunity for you.

3. Authentic Content Marketing

My favorite way to build credibility is to create and share authentic, relevant, consistent content. As you might know, this is what I teach and try my best to model.

If you do <u>authentic content marketing</u>, you are continually showing up to your audience as someone who cares about helping them. This builds your credibility over time.

Also, you are making it easier for people to spread the word about you. **The easiest way for anyone to refer you is to share your free content with their friends.**

The challenge with authentic content marketing is that it takes time until it starts to work its magic. It usually takes a few months at least. Yet, when it starts to work, it's amazing and totally worthwhile.

In 2014 I started creating content, but not consistently. Then I started doing content consistently in mid-2015. After about a year, I noticed that I was no longer needing to seek out clients... all new clients were coming to me on their own initiative, thanks to my content.

I haven't needed to reach out for new clients since 2016. I have a consistently full practice, with a waiting list. This wasn't true from 2009-2015 when I was only doing launches, but not creating content consistently.

It is never too early (or late) to start.

Look at the 3 sections above -- Audience, Pricing, Credibility -- and ask yourself which one(s) are important for your situation now?

Pick one, then try the solutions I've described.

I look forward to hearing how it goes for you.

Share this chapter, or to comment on it, using this link: https://www.georgekao.com/blog/what-to-do-when-not-enough-people-are-signing-up-for-your-services

Section 4:

Authentic Networking

Chapter 22: How to Keep in Touch with Previous Clients

When was the last time you reached out to previous clients about possibly working with you again?

If your clients needed your services in the past, they'll probably need them again.

And some of your previous clients will want to refer a friend or colleague to you… if only you were at the top of their mind.

Ask if they'd like to receive your email newsletter

When a client first begins to work with you, ask whether they'd like to receive your ongoing email newsletter (if they aren't already subscribed.)

If they enjoy your newsletter, they're probably going to stay subscribed, even after completing their client engagement with you. This is the easiest way for you to keep in touch with all your previous clients at once.

Didn't get a chance to ask? It's not too late. Email them a sample newsletter now, and ask if they'd like to receive it going forward. If so, add them yourself, to be sure they're subscribed.

You can also send this kind of email to your *potential* clients—those who have inquired about working with you — because if they're interested in your services, they'll likely be interested in your newsletter.

I've worked with hundreds of service providers over the years, and almost *none* of them have done this simple thing of checking whether I'm on their email newsletter or not, and if not, whether I'd like to receive it.

Another thing that almost no one does is to check in with their previous clients personally.

Connect with them occasionally and personally

Here's a simple plan for the outreach:

1. Write down a list of past clients. Sort the list by the clients you *most* enjoyed working with. Start your outreach at the top of the list.

2. For each client, first go to their social media profile, blog, newsletter, or podcast—wherever they have been active— and find something you appreciate. Maybe they posted a question that you can answer. Maybe they posted some

content you'd like to re-share on your social media and if so, mention/tag them in appreciation.

3. Write a personal email to them. Consider including some or all of the following elements…

Let them know that they came to mind… and that you enjoyed seeing their recent social media update/newsletter/etc.

Mention how much you enjoyed working with them before. List a few things you were glad to have done in your work together in the past, as a celebration or reminder of progress.

Mention you have a couple of open spots to serve clients right now and if they are interested in continuing your work together, that you'd welcome it.

List a few things you've been working with your current clients on (keeping those clients anonymous of course). And send them a link to an article you wrote or video you made, that you think will be relevant for them.

End the email saying that no matter what, they are always welcome to reach out to you with any questions—and you'd love to help.

You don't have to include all the elements above.

*Just sending a thoughtful personal email is going above and beyond other service providers who, by and large, are **not** keeping in touch!*

If you've had previous email thread(s) with them, consider replying to one of those, with some of the above elements.

(If your client replies, and it results in an email dialogue about issues that should be discussed in your capacity as their coach/consultant, invite them to a 30 minute phone call that will serve as an exploratory session about whether to continue working with you.)

With this kind of personal outreach, you'll certainly stand out as one of the few providers in your clients' lives that are thoughtful enough to keep in touch.

Keep expectations light

The idea is to keep in touch as a reminder, as a courtesy, without attachment to whether they will continue to work with you.

Most will be glad to hear from you.

If your email doesn't get a response, then you might want to keep in touch less frequently with that person, but still touch in every now and then, if you had indeed enjoyed your work with them.

Bless and then let go. Give some space, and then connect thoughtfully again at a future date.

Share this chapter, or to comment on it, using this link:
https://medium.com/@georgekao/are-you-keeping-in-touch-with-previous-clients-2b1060df8d62

Chapter 23: Seeking Referrals from Your Warm Connectors

Your warm connectors are people you know—hence "warm"—and who enjoy helping/connecting people—hence "connectors."

You probably know at least a dozen such people, maybe more.

Start making a list. Sources to look for your warm connectors include:

- Your email "sent" folder (people you've sent emails to)
- Your mobile phone history (whom you've called or texted)
- Your LinkedIn contacts
- Your list of Facebook friends and perhaps also your followers
- Your Twitter followers
- Perhaps you have a spreadsheet or other way of listing your contacts

When was the last time you reached out to your warm connectors about referring business to you?

Most business owners neglect this simple, yet effective method. If you do this regularly, and thoughtfully—with the intention to help your connectors—you'll be top-of-mind for them.

...and you'll likely get new client referrals.

Elements of a good referral request email:

- Friendliness & Conciseness
- List the few key problems that your ideal clients would love help with
- A few of your best <u>credibility indicators</u>
- Offer the referee (the potential client) something useful e.g. free 30-minute exploratory/coaching call, a useful article or video, etc.
- If appropriate, offer some incentive for a successful referral, such as: a free session, a discount on your services, commission, a donation to their favorite charity, a gift certificate to their favorite restaurant.
- Be clear how you want them to refer you (e.g. "I'd be very grateful if you can think of 3 people to forward this email onto.")
- Say you're open to helping them too—and truly mean it! Be specific if you can.

Here is a sample email:

Subject Line Ideas:

- know someone who wants to grow their business?
- [Referral Request] Friends who want to grow their business

Email Body:

Hi [Name],

I hope your week is going well!

[Here, give them a genuine appreciation for something they posted on social media recently, or their newsletter, or if they've been looking for a resource, share your suggestions with them.]

Today I'm reaching out to see if you know any Coaches or Healers who are passionately wanting to grow their business. I just opened up new availability in my 1–1 marketing coaching.

(Please reply and let me know how your [business] is doing—how can I help?)

I love guiding business owners into:

* creating online offerings so they can reach a bigger audience
* being found by their ideal clients online
* scaling up their income by enrolling more (or higher-end) clients

* simplifying the technologies they actually need, including social media, and showing them how to use it mindfully

A couple of recent clients have said this about me:

- "George Kao's coaching has been a lot more effective than any of the other business coaching I've invested in."
- "George's solid expertise in marketing along with his hands-on support have been instrumental in helping me actualize my heart's desire."

…see more of my client reviews at:

www.georgekao.com/coaching

I would be very grateful if there were 2 friends you could forward this email to, or make a quick email intro and I will follow up with them.

They can find lots of helpful free content at www.georgekao.com/knowledge— or for my services, have them check out

www.georgekao.com/services

If they are considering hiring a business coach, I'd love to offer them 30 minutes of free private coaching—whether or not they sign up with me. The call is about helping them. I spend only a few minutes at the end of the call answering any questions they have about my services. To schedule the free coaching, have them go here: [the link to your scheduling system.]

> Given the values you and I both share —integrity, authenticity, generosity—your referrals will likely resonate with me as well. I will take great care of them.
>
> What about you? Reply and let me know what you're working on [if you can, mention a specific project you know they were working on] and how I might support you!
>
> In Service,
>
> George

Another example, adapted from the book $100 Startup by Chris Guillebeau:

> I wanted to let you know about a new project I'm working on.
>
> It's called ..... And it's meant to serve (type of person) to help them (main benefit).
>
> It's important to them / now because ...
>
> If you like the idea and would like to help, here is what I'm needing at this time:
>
> Action Option 1
>
> Action Option 2
>
> Eg introductions to (referral partners)
>
> Send this link to 3 people who could benefit as I'm giving away (comp session)

Join my newsletter to keep updated and get (content)

Thanks for your time!

Another example, used with permission from audio business coach Nathan Lively:

> Hi [person],
>
> [A paragraph of personal connection first, e.g. "How's it going with your job? How's the family doing?" ...but being a bit more specific is better. Really do care!]
>
> Hey I'm looking for more clients for my coaching program. Is it cool if I tell you little bit about it to see if you might know anyone who would be interested?
>
> The person writes back "Sure!"
>
> Nathan sends back an email with more info, like the sample I already shared above.
>
> If the person comes back and says not sure how to refer people, Nathan sends a more simple guidance on how to refer. Here's his version:
>
> Well, I know you run into a lot of audio people and I think this would be something perfect for you to have in your bag when someone says,
>
> * Do you know how I can find more work? OR
> * I'm in corporate audio right now but I'd like to move into concert audio. OR

> * I'd like to grow my business, but I'm not sure what to do.
>
> They can find lots of helpful free content at sounddesignlive.com/archives—or for my personal support, have them check out sounddesignlive.com/coaching.
>
> Thanks Pete!

Just as important as sending referral requests is to Send Gratitude, and to Follow Up:

- Send a personal thank-you email to everyone who replies.

- Send a follow-up request, for example every 6-12 months, or for those who refer, follow up every 3-6 months with gratitude and updates re: their previous referral.

- Most business owners don't even request referrals, let alone follow-up. If you do both (and do it courteously, thoughtfully) you are going to be top-of-mind and get the referrals.

Here's an example of a follow-up email, used with Doug's permission:

> I am following up in keeping with my intention after speaking with you of checking in from time to time. I wanted to let you know that I have 10 open

coaching slots for February for complimentary 30 minute "Expand Your Reach" sessions to see if it would be a good fit. If you know anyone who is looking for another way to get their message out in the world, I would definitely love to speak with them. The best way to reach me is through [Doug shared his email; instead I'll share his public FB page.] Things are going really well with coaching! Right now at least 2 of the top 10 podcasts in self-help, health, kids and family and spirituality and religion on iTunes New and Noteworthy are from my client community.

How are things going for you? Definitely let me know when you are opening your coaching program again. Also, would love to have you back on The Coachzing Show!

If you have received any effective emails that has gotten you to refer clients to someone, or if you yourself have sent an effective email, I would love to know!

Share this chapter, or to comment on it, using this link: https://medium.com/@georgekao/sample-email-to-warm-connectors-about-referring-new-clients-dc9959e4b5f0

Chapter 24: Who Are Your "Niche Mates"?

We get fearful when we think of our "competition"—they could "crush" us, or at least, make us work a lot harder than we need to.

Instead, let's remember that they, too, have families to feed, dreams they hope to achieve, and unknown suffering in their life that would inspire our compassion.

Let's think of them as "niche mates"—occupying the same niche as us.

We have 3 options:

1. We can fight each other for business, resulting in discouragement, avoidance, or aggression.
2. We can learn from each other, since we are trying to serve similar people with our similar skills.
3. If we get creative, we can figure out a way to grow together by partnering in some way.

People don't usually think about this. They get swept up by fear, and default to either avoidance or aggression.

They might get "strategic" and sometimes try to learn from their competition, but even so, it's often out of negativity, hoping the competition eventually goes down.

I encourage you to be mindful when you catch yourself feeling fear of your competitors. Direct your energy consciously toward **learning** or **partnering**.

The labels we use influence how we think about others. Let's refrain from the term "competitor" (aggression) and instead replace it with the term "niche mate" (suggesting collaboration.)

Find a win-win relationship

Every single business can have enough clients, when we each became more mindful, active, and caring about creating win-win relationships.

A niche mate is another business, like you, that provides a service that is similar to what you provide, and they might even serve the same type of audience.

A niche mate, like you, has both insecurities and genius zones (that might complement yours). Like you, they also need to support themselves and maybe a family too. A niche mate also deserves opportunities to succeed. Like you, a niche mate also needs help.

In fact, your niche mates are either your best mirrors, or your best partners.

Niche Mates as Mirrors

It's difficult to see how good (or bad) you look, and adjust yourself accordingly, unless you look into a mirror.

Similarly, it's hard to figure out the best ways to improve your own branding, messaging, and marketing, unless you look at your niche mates. They essentially serve as mirrors for your business.

When you look at a business that provides a similar service as you, you're naturally more able to critique or praise how they're marketing or running their business.

Do you *love* something they're doing? Do more of it yourself. (Not copying, but seeing how you could do the same kind of thing in your own style, with your own voice.)

Do you *dislike* something they're doing? Take that criticism and refrain from doing it in your own business, too.

Study Your Niche Mates

Who are your niche mates? Ask around your network for who else does similar work that you do.

Use Google to find more niche mates.

Write down 5 niche mates that are most similar to what you do.

For each one, answer these questions:

- What are 2 things you like about their services that you might want to emulate?
- What's broken? What's missing? What's unnecessary?
- What's unique about your services that makes you distinct from them?
- What are 2 things you like about their marketing?
- What are 2 things you *don't* like about their marketing?
- What's unique about your marketing that makes you distinct from them?
- Are you addressing the same audience? Or what's different about yours?
- What could they be doing differently or better to meet their audience's needs?

From these insights, modify and improve your own business and marketing!

Instead of copying, focus on being of Service…

Don't try to match your niche mates' offerings, feature by feature. Instead, for each feature they provide, ask how it tries to solve a problem for clients.

Ask yourself:

- Is there a better way to solve this problem?
- Can I solve it in a different way, in my own style, with my own experience and wisdom?
- Can I solve it in a way that is more effective or delightful, based on what I know about my clients?

Focus on solving your ideal clients' challenges by meeting their needs in the way way you know.

Niche Mates as Partners

Contact your niche mates casually, to see if they might be open to finding ways to collaborate or mutually support each other.

Some people might not respond at all. However, the ones who do respond positively, are abundance-minded as you are. Perhaps a future friend!

Why our niche mates can be some of our best partners:

Do your offerings complement each other? Do you help your audiences in different ways or styles?

Statistically, your own audience has some people who don't (and will never) buy from you—and this is also true of any niche mate you talk to. Yet, those same non-buyers may love to buy from *your* niche mate if they are endorsed by you… and vice versa… some of their non-buying audience may love to buy from you. In other words, you might be able to refer a lot of business to each other!

Help one another by introducing your content or offerings to each other's audience, so that everyone can be helped:

- That audience is helped by having an option that may work better for them
- The niche mate who makes a sale is helped with getting a new client (or at least, a new reader/viewer)
- The introducer benefits by building trust with all parties involved
- The person who buys something is likely to buy another thing similar to it. The person who likes reading a particular topic is likely to enjoy finding out about someone else writing about that topic.

Partnering with appropriate and willing niche mates can be a win for everyone.

In your research into niche mates, also take note of who is partnering with your niche mates? Who is endorsing or recommending them? They might also be interested in introducing you.

When we connect and share, there is more than enough for everyone.

Always remember:

Through the internet, the world is so large that there are always more than enough ideal clients for you. We simply need to be more mindful, active, and caring in connecting with our niche mates.

There are no competitors. Only mirrors to respect and learn from, or partners to work with!

Share this chapter, or comment on it, using this link:
https://medium.com/@georgekao/see-competitors-as-niche-mates-instead-b83830229f72

Chapter 25: Trading Content Promotions

I wish more heart-based entrepreneurs would reach out to one another and form collaborations. When it's the right fit, it is magical. Everybody wins!

Here's an example:

Jason is an energy healer. Sarah is a work-life balance coach. They've seen each other in a Facebook group, and enjoyed each other's comments.

Jason and Sarah each have a small audience, with 100 email subscribers each.
Is there a simple way to collaborate where **both** can grow their email lists? Yes.

Jason takes a few minutes to research Sarah's content -- and he notices that she is an expert on the topic of Self-Care, which Jason's audience would probably love to learn about. And, it looks like Sarah doesn't talk about Energy Healing (which her audience would likely appreciate), which happens to be Jason's expertise.

In other words, there's a clear opportunity to benefit **both** audiences if they each bring their respective expertise to the other audience... as long as the topics they choose are complementary.

And as they promote each other's content, they will each grow their audiences. What used to be a 100-person email list becomes 110, or more. Everybody wins: the audiences get the benefit of new and relevant knowledge and the hosts grow their audiences. Trust grows for all parties involved.

Back to our example:

After Jason researches Sarah's online presence, he messages her...

"Sarah, I've been enjoying your thoughtful comments in [Group]! I was checking out some of your content on your Facebook page, and love your perspective and tips about Self-Care. This isn't something I've talked much with my audience about... and yet it's such an important topic. Also, I noticed you haven't talked much with your audience about how Energy Healing can be a powerful support for their self-care and work-life balance. This happens to be my area of passion and expertise. I wonder if we could collaborate... perhaps I can host you on a webinar to my audience where you teach your expertise of self-care? And in turn you can host me on a webinar to your people where I explain and offer an experience of energy healing? I believe both

audiences would enjoy it, and we'll also grow our audience as a result. As a thank-you, I'd also enjoy gifting you a private session of Energy Healing, if you're up for it. Looking forward to your thoughts. Either way, I appreciate that you're out there doing great work."

NOTE: Don't copy-and-paste the above template, because that's the definition of inauthentic networking! Instead, sleep on it, and then without looking at the above, write your own version in your own voice. Just imagine you are reaching out to a new friend... how would you speak?

To complete our example:

Sarah and Jason promote each other's webinars to their respective audiences. Even though their email lists are only 100 people each, they can also do some personal outreach to their network to bring a few more people to the webinars they're promoting.

As a result, after this simple collaboration they're likely going to each have more email subscribers!

So the question for you is -- how many collaborations can you do?

There are almost unlimited opportunities. Start looking for compatible colleagues.

To be clear, I'm not suggesting co-teaching or co-creating content yet... that's a more challenging collaboration. In our simple example, which I recommend everyone start with -- Jason simply introduces Sarah at the beginning of her webinar (to Jason's audience) and allows Sarah to do her magic. Same thing when Sarah promotes and introduces Jason to her audience: Jason gets to be the expert during his hour with Sarah's audience.

Important consideration for a truly win-win collaboration:

It has to make sense to *the audience* why the Host is promoting the Expert.

Energy Healing and Self-Care happen to be complementary topics, so both audiences can clearly see the relevance of the Host's introduction of the Expert.

But let's say Sarah was a career coach, not a self-care coach... now it might be too much of a stretch for Jason the energy healer to promote Sarah the career coach.

However, they can still be of mutual support, by introducing each other to related colleagues. They can help expand each other's networks that way.

Each person should care about their relationship to the audience and be a relevant curator for them, not promoting stuff all over the place, doing all kinds of random collaborations for the sake of "growing their list".

Besides topic-compatibility, another factor is audience-size-compatibility.

Unless you already have a huge audience, don't expect to go to Brene Brown and have a cross-promotion opportunity. However, Brene might partner with Oprah, given compatibilities of topic and audience-size.

So I recommend that you start with colleagues whose audience size is similar size to yours... how similar is up to your courage, or compassion.

A few ways to guess someone's audience size:
- FB Fan Page following
- Twitter following
- Instagram following
- On their website, they might even say how many email subscribers they have

If you are interested in growing your audience, I really encourage you to put these thoughts into practice. This is a proven method I have used for years to grow my audience, and many other successful colleagues also do this often.

In the marketing world, this type of collaboration has many names:
- JV's (joint ventures)
- promotional (promo) partnerships
- strategic alliances
- guest posting (here I'm talking about doing it mutually)
- "collabs" (what Youtubers call it when they do this type of content exchange)
- #share4share is what Instagrammers call it

Remember to take at least a few minutes to research your potential collaborator, to gauge the topic-compatibility and audience-size. If it's a good fit, then everybody wins.

Too few people are reaching out to each other. Be the one that builds more connections in your community.

Share this chapter, or comment on it, using this link:
https://www.facebook.com/GeorgeKaoCommunity/videos/10156614241599867/

Chapter 26: Trading Services for Feedback & Referrals

It is important to keep practicing your skills, to keep applying it in different client situations, to deepen both your self-knowledge and awareness of the current market.

Consider the idea that you can become a true master of anything by practicing it for approximately 10,000 hours. Whether that number is accurate it or not, the kernel of truth remains: continuous practice will improve your skills.

You probably don't need another certificate or training program. See my blog post about <u>breaking the pattern of delay in your business</u>.

What will likely help the most is to keep using your skills, day by day, to become so excellent at what you do, that clients just can't help but refer you to their friends.

If you've got a lot of client openings right now, consider doing this:

Trade sessions with other service providers for feedback.

This allows you to use your time wisely, by continuing to practice your craft, while getting to know colleagues who might become referral sources.

Here are the steps:

STEP 1.

Look at your network and write down the names of your colleagues/friends who meet these 3 criteria:
- They are also service providers.
- They might be looking for more clients, and might be open to trading with you.
- They have a network (of friends or colleagues) similar to your ideal clients.

The easiest way to look at your network might be to go to your LinkedIn Connections. Underneath each name is their professional headline.

If you don't have any Linkedin Connections, check out your Facebook list of friends.

STEP 2.

Contact the ones that meet all 3 criteria above, and offer to trade 1–2 sessions with them, so that you can:

- Give each other thoughtful feedback on what's working well, or what might be improved.
- Potentially become referral sources for each other.
- If it feels right and appropriate, give a testimonial to each other, which can then be posted as a LinkedIn Recommendation, Facebook Review, Google Business Review, and, if the business has a physical office, a Yelp Review as well. This will improve your online presence.

STEP 3.

Schedule and do those traded sessions. Make it a *real* session that you would do for a client, not just an exploratory/discovery call.

Give each other thoughtful feedback on what worked well, and what can be improved.

STEP 4.

If you really liked their service, take the initiative and offer them a testimonial. The best is a short video. If you're not comfortable on video, a written testimonial can still be very helpful.

Let them know they are welcome to put it on their website, and ask if they would like you to also post it elsewhere, e.g.

as a LinkedIn recommendation, a Review on their Facebook Business Page, or a Review on their Google Business Page.

STEP 5.

Ask them if any of their friends/colleagues come to mind that you can also trade with.

If you liked their service, also take the initiative to look through your own network for colleagues to introduce to them.

Be sure to ask your friends, before you make an introduction to them. Let's say you just traded sessions with Anne, and you'd like to introduce her to Bob, Claire, and David. Send Anne a brief email that includes the names, websites (if available) and any relevant info about Bob, Claire, David. Ask whom she'd like to be introduced to. Let's say Anne picks Claire and David. Then you should individually email Claire, and David, separately, and give them info about Anne and see if they'd like to be introduced. Only when both parties say Yes, do you make the introduction. This is good networking etiquette that a lot of people forget to follow.

If these steps resonate with you, go ahead and apply them, and let me know how it goes!

You could even comment on this companion FB video, to trade with others who might be reading this chapter.

May this method bring you mutually-supportive connections!

Chapter 27: Reaching Out to Group Owners/Admins

A rarely used technique for connecting with potential new clients is to be endorsed in an online group--by the owner herself.

Here are the steps to making it work:

STEP 1. Add your ideal clients as friends on Facebook and LinkedIn.

(Your ideal clients are current clients who are receiving the most benefit from working with you, or previous clients whom you loved working with. They could also be friends or acquaintances who you'd imagine to be great clients.)

STEP 2. Check out their online group involvement.

On Facebook you can do this by going to their profile, click "More" (next to "About" and "Friends") and clicking Groups.

On LinkedIn you can go to their profile, scroll all the way down, and see what LinkedIn groups they've joined.

The fact that your ideal client is in those groups means that there are probably other members who are similar to your ideal client!

STEP 3. Bookmark (or join) the groups that are most relevant for your expertise.

Out of all these groups, which are likely to have discussions where your expertise would be helpful?

Or which groups would be appropriate for posting your content, if the group rules allow it?

STEP 4. For the groups you've chosen, contact the group owner or manager and offer yourself as an expert resource on your topic.

Privately message the group owner, either through Facebook private message, LinkedIn private message, or by looking up their contact info online.

Tell them (1) you are glad they created a group that supports so many people, and that (2) one of your ideal clients is in their group (keep their name anonymous), and chances are that others in the group would benefit from your expertise as well. (3) Let them know if they receive any questions or requests for help regarding your expertise, to feel free to send them to you. (4) Tell them you will do your best to help anyone who contacts you, and that if they need a service provider you will help them find the perfect fit, whether it's you or a colleague.

***

Imagine if you do the 4 steps above. Let's say you have 10 ideal clients whose profiles you're looking at, and that each of those 10 clients has joined 5 online groups that are relevant for you. That's 50 group owners for you to contact.

Imagine contacting two of them per week. This allows you to contact 50 group owners in 6 months. Then, start over and follow-up with those 50, so that they are hearing from you twice a year... which is not too often.

Again, make your outreach message to those group owners generous-in-heart, being of true service, not trying to sell your service. Be a genuine resource for their people, about your expertise.

Imagine out of 50 group owners, 5 of them referred 2 new clients to you each time you contacted them. This would equate to 20 new clients every year, from this strategy alone.

Try it out, keep tweaking your outreach message as you go along, and let me know how it goes for you!

Section 5:

Pep Talk

Chapter 28: Your Outreach is a Blessing, not a Bother

It is natural to feel shy about reaching out to prospective clients, or even to previous clients.

Since you're reading this book, I'm guessing that you are a natural giver. Maybe you aren't accustomed to reaching out to your network about your latest offerings.

Try this reframe:

You aren't selling them. And you aren't asking them for a favor. You are giving them (or someone they know) the chance to receive support for their problems or goals.

If they are a potential referral source, you are giving them the opportunity to be a blessing to the others that they will introduce to you.

This is really the way I look at it -- *You are a blessing to those you are reaching out to.*

Your outreach is a blessing to them, if they indeed need what you offer, or if they know someone who does.

I'm not asking you to *make* yourself believe it, by using affirmations, etc. If that helps, sure you can go ahead and use such tools.

What I *am* saying is that this *is* the actual reality: by reaching out to someone who needs what you have, or know people who need it, you are in fact being a blessing to them, especially if you reach out to the right people in a service-oriented way.

They won't think "why are you bothering me" but rather, "How come you didn't tell me sooner?"

Or they might say "I had forgotten that's what you do… thanks for reminding me!"

When you reach out to your warm contacts, and allow them to spread the word about your services, you are also giving them the chance to give back to you.

If you've been of service to them, they have a feeling of gratitude toward you that, up to this point, hasn't had much of an outlet. You probably have a giving tendency, and are not so great at allowing your friends to give to you. This is that chance for them to show you that they care, to reciprocate for your caring.

Give your friends and colleagues the chance to finally use your services. Or to be a connector (and therefore a blessing) to others who need what you do.

This is not a "favor" for you. You are a blessing to them. Allow this opportunity. Start your outreach!

Share this chapter, or to comment, using this link:
https://www.facebook.com/GeorgeKaoCommunity/posts/10156434072874867/

Chapter 29: Consistent Income Requires Consistent Output

If you're seeking consistent income, aim for consistent valuable output:

1. Are you <u>consistently creating authentic, relevant content</u>?
2. Are you <u>consistently connecting with new referral sources</u>?
3. Are you <u>consistently testing new low-price offers</u>?
4. Are you <u>consistently reaching out for clients</u>?

Doing at least 2 of these four strategies, consistently and skillfully, will give you a very good chance of creating consistent income.

How do you become skillful?

It requires your consistent practice, and willingness to make mistakes and learn from "failure." (It's no failure if you learn, and if you keep going!) Make consistent effort in a useful direction.

In other words, are you being <u>truly productive</u> on a consistent basis?

You'll notice that one key aspect of the above actions is that they are always done *in relationship to others, rather than working in isolation* You're always getting feedback from others so you can see whether you are putting out value, not just fluff.

Eventually, the valuable output in your business can be <u>outsourced or automated</u>, (e.g. selling online courses using paid ads managed by a savvy VA.) However, until then, it is up to you—the business creator—to create value on a consistent basis if you expect consistent income.

If your business isn't getting consistent income, your business isn't putting out consistent value.

Here is the story of my own business consistency:

In the first five years of my business, I created consistent income by doing consistent launches of my services & programs. On average, I was presenting about 2 webinars per month, often to new audiences, through different joint venture (JV) partners.

I was creating a lot of consistent income, but it required consistent selling on those webinars.

In 2014, I stopped my launches because I was getting tired of selling. Instead, I started a totally different strategy:

creating authentic, relevant, consistent content. I created 70 youtube videos that year. That gave me some initial practice into content creation.

In 2015 I committed to creating 100 videos. Doing so has made a significant difference in my skillfulness and willingness to create consistent, authentic, relevant content. (Here's my 100th video!)

Since that time, I've continued publishing 2-3 videos per week (as well as written blog posts alongside those videos). I do this consistently, all year long, except for Christmas holiday week.

In the middle of 2016 I noticed that I had no more room in my business coaching practice—and yet I had *not* needed to reach out to clients for months! (In the past, I had to keep launching/announcing my coaching programs all year long.)

To add to this: in 2017 I started consistently offering a monthly online workshop on a different topic each month. This is gently announced in my weekly email newsletter, and sent to my workshops email list (I send 2 emails compared to peers who often send 5-10 emails announcing each event!), and through Facebook ads.

In 2018 I added a new consistent valuable output: Publishing 2 books per year. I have an [Amazon Author page](#) now.

As a result? I've had stable income for years, because I've been consistently creating valuable output in various ways.

Here is the bottom line:

If your business income is not steady and reliable, your business output is not steady and reliable.

Take a look at the 4 strategies shared at the top of this chapter. Which ones will you commit to becoming consistent with moving forward?

Once you choose a consistent rhythm that works for you, and work that rhythm, I promise you that you'll be on a solid path to consistent income.

🍵

Share this chapter, or comment on it, using this link: https://medium.com/@georgekao/want-consistent-income-have-consistent-output-720467baaaeb

Chapter 30: To Go Big, Think Small

What is your business goal?

Is it some big financial number (e.g. $10,000 per month or more) that seems far off from your current situation?

Intimidating goals can spawn anxiety, overthinking, and procrastination. You keep thinking (subconsciously) "I'm still not there yet… I'm still not enough."

Or you'll continually doubt your own plans: "What if this strategy isn't enough to create that dream result?"

Another problem is that thinking of big money tends to make humans anti-social. This limits your ability to create helpful relationships.

Similarly, I don't recommend having a huge audience goal like 10,000 email list subscribers (if you're still far off from there) because again, it can cause anxiety. You'll also be tempted to make short-term marketing decisions to "get" subscribers, in ways that may be manipulative or otherwise damaging to your reputation.

Instead of always thinking of big goals, try focusing daily on the doable steps that are pointed toward the bigger goal.

By focusing on completing the small goals each day, the big goal will take care of itself.

In fact, I encourage you to connect your big goal to *a heartfelt vision* for the world.
And connect your small daily goal to your values, e.g. service, love, wisdom.

Step 1: Clarify your big goal, and connect it to a heartfelt vision.

It's fine to start by defining a big goal. And then, connect it to a vision that uplifts your soul and makes your heart sing, so that you can align your whole being in one beneficent direction.

"I wish to earn $10,000/month, working no more than 30 hours a week, in order to spend more time loving my family, and supporting the people in my community."

"I wish to have 1,000 real Facebook fans who engage, so that I can more effectively contribute to the spread of hope, love, and wisdom online."

Step 2: Define milestones (think smaller).

Break the big goal into the most doable milestones. If $10,000/mo is the big goal, then the first milestone might be $2,500/month.

Now think smaller:
- $2,500/month = $500/mo x 5 Clients

If you have zero clients right now, think even smaller:
- Acquire 1 Client at $500/month… then repeat that 5 times.

Other examples:
- If getting 5 new clients is daunting, then this may be more doable: 3 new clients + 2 previous clients who renew.
- $2,500 / mo = 25 billable hours per month (assuming $100/hour) = 6 billable hours per week, so focus on getting those 6 billable hours each week.

Step 3: Plan consistent actions, connected to your values.

Based on your own life experience, as well as conversations with friends, colleagues, and a coach if you have one, figure out the plan of consistent action that you can commit to taking.

A simple example would be to contact 10 potential clients per month, if you are able to commit to that. 10 potential clients per month, depending on your quality of contact method, may lead to 3 exploratory calls, which may then land you 1 new client.

Again, think smaller: 10 contacts per month means 3-4 contacts per week. That is definitely doable. If you work M, W, F, then make it an even more doable goal and think "1 to 2 contacts per working day."

Be sure to connect that daily action to your values, so that it's an action you can really believe in, and continuing to fulfill your life purpose everyday, even if the action seems small.

For example: "I'm contacting potential clients from an energetic space of serving rather than selling."

Instead of thinking of "playing a bigger game" let's aim to "play a deeper game, everyday."

Step 4: Be sure you are consistent in those planned actions.

If you are consistent in your actions, you'll learn much faster. You'll rapidly grow your skills.

With better skill comes better results. This is why consistency is so important.
To stay consistent, you may need to find a motivational method that works for you. Here are 7 examples:
7 Motivational Methods to Help You Overcome Procrastination and Get Focused

---

Step 5: Be willing to change your goals or actions. Everything is learning.

What if you start climbing a ladder, and find that it's placed on the wrong wall? Get back down and try a different ladder.

Same with your big or small goals: If you go in one direction and find that it's not aligning with your purpose, change directions.

The tricky part is to know when to persist, versus when you need to keep going. I can't give you the "right" answer. It will come with life experience. Get the perspective of the trusted advisors in your life.

Then make the decision to persist or change, and then learn from it.

Do the 5 steps above make sense to you? Any questions? Feel free to ask.

Share this chapter, or comment on it, using this link:
https://medium.com/p/to-go-big-think-small-c6565718cbc1

Chapter 31: Sell Only to Those Who Care

Trying hard to persuade people is what spawns inauthenticity.

Many of us dislike marketing & selling because it often feels inauthentic.

When you're in the energy of trying to "get" an unwilling person to believe you, and to buy your thing, it's easy to slip into saying anything you think the other person wants to hear. You lose your grounding and authenticity.

Instead, what if you sell only to people who will quickly believe the value of what you're selling?

When speaking to potential clients, only describe your services to the interested.

When creating an email or webpage to describe your product / service / program, picture in your mind those who would be eagerly on board, if only they knew about the offering.

Create a Facebook event page for the people who would be eager to attend, if only they knew about it.

Do this, and your marketing/selling will feel like joyful connection, rather than a necessary evil.

It's Your Ivy League Program

This applies whether you're selling a $60 online workshop (my examples) , or if you're selling a premium high-end program.

I was consulting with someone who is selling her $12,000 coaching program. She felt nervous about how to convince others of the value of such a program. I said:

"If you were interested in going to Harvard University, would they need to convince you of the value of their program?

Harvard would be many times more expensive than her program.

If you have a premium program, think of it like an ivy league education for your ideal client.

If you create a program you really believe has value, and you describe it in that kind of way to the ideal client, then if anything, they would have to convince you to let them in, not the other way around.

It's Your Black Friday Offering

If you have a low-price offering (e.g. an online course) think about your ideal buyer like they are waiting for Black Friday to finally get such a great deal on a product they've been wanting. (Not that you have to discount, but I'm talking about that kind of right-match and eagerness.)

Sell To The Eager 10%

When you do your overall marketing, sell to the 10% most eager ones in your audience. Think of them. Write your marketing copy for them.

You can be in your authentic self, joyfully sharing what you have thoughtfully put together. Ideal clients / customers are eager looking forward to your offering your product or service!

Sell only to those who know the value. Remind them of it. Clarify anything that's not obvious. They'll be glad to see your offer. They are happy that it exists because it's something they've been looking for.

Lack of sales—What to do?

If not enough people know the value, don't push, or you'll go into desperation and neediness.

As you push, you will push people away.

If you're lacking enough sales of your product / service / program, here are 3 helpful actions to take:

Do additional "fan interviews" as described in this post:
https://www.georgekao.com/Blog/PassionCompassion

Have conversations with more people from your existing audience, so that you can understand more deeply what they're wanting at this time.

This then allows you to create or modify your product or program into something of which they would already understand the value, rather than trying to sell them something they don't yet value.

Authentic Content Marketing

Spend more time with your authentic content marketing so that your ideal audience can find you.

Share your vision widely and deeply, without attachment or resentment, rather with a desire to connect with the kindred spirits that are out there.

It can speed up your efforts by a lot if you are willing to spend $30 per month on Facebook Ads. Generally the more you can spend the faster you will reach the people who want your offerings. If you'd like to learn from me how to use Facebook Ads effectively, take my online course: <u>Facebook Marketing for Authentic Business</u>

Authentic Collaborations

Spend more time connecting with relevant influencers who have the audience you'd love to reach.

Their audience, if it's ideal for your offering, would love to find out about it.

You might then pay a commission to that influencer for any sales that result. It can be a true win-win.

Remember <u>your true fans</u>.

If you keep <u>caring about them</u>, more than other businesses are willing to care, they will gladly buy from you. Or, they will help you by telling you what to sell to them and to others just like them.

To grow your authentic business, keep caring, connecting, and creating offerings from that love and understanding.

Can you tell me something about yourself?

One of the strange things about writing a book — instead of having a conversation — is that I don't know the person I'm "talking" to through this book.

Can you let me know a bit about you?

To help me with this, take a moment to fill out this short form:
www.GeorgeKao.com/BookSurvey

I personally read every response.

Upon submitting the form, you'll also see some bonus content related to this book!

Sincere Thanks,
George Kao

Acknowledgements

These kind souls helped me edit this book: Dianne Allen, Sharon Rosen, Rochelle Melander, Nick Ward, Jenn Simpson, Jakki Francis, Paolo Donati, Martha Winterhalter, Matthea Osinga, Colette Van Heerden, Reza Garajedaghi, Cristina Maria Costa Machado.

Thank you!

I also offer my thanks to my MasterHeart Group clients, as well as my Facebook Page commenters, who gave their impressions of the book's cover designs.

To all of my clients: I honor the work you do. Your dedication to continue improving your authentic business is inspiring!

To my students: Thank you for your sincere engagement with the material, and your thoughtful questions. You are helping me create better courses to serve you and fellow students.

To those who watch my videos and read my posts: Each time I see your views, likes and comments, it encourages me, and inspires me to become more effective in serving you.

Your questions and comments have helped to make the content of this book.

To my referral partners: I'm deeply grateful for your trust in my ability to help those you send to me. I'll continue to do my best to make you proud!

Lastly, to my wife: My heartfelt gratitude for your loyal support and love. You provide an amazing foundation for my joyful productivity.

About The Author

Since 2009, George Kao has been a marketing mentor, consultant, and coach to thousands of small business owners, speakers, and authors.

George's mission is to raise the marketing effectiveness of those who prioritize integrity, compassion, and generosity in their business.

George teaches online courses about authentic online marketing, including Facebook Advertising, Google Advertising, authentic content creation, defining your core message, how to create and market courses, and joyful productivity. You can find his courses at www.GeorgeKao.com/Workshops

George works with a few 1-1 clients at a time to help them stabilize their income, expand their visibility authentically, and structure their business so that they can experience more freedom and joy in their work. As of 2016, his 1-1 coaching practice has been consistently full. If interested in inquiring about the waiting list, go to www.GeorgeKao.com/Coaching

To receive a regular email newsletter with George Kao's recent and best articles, visit
www.GeorgeKao.com/newsletter

www.ingramcontent.com/pod-product-compliance
Lightning Source LLC
Chambersburg PA
CBHW031926240526
45464CB00023B/1699